Creative
BLACKSMITHING

Creative
BLACKSMITHING

Peat Oberon

THE CROWOOD PRESS

First published in 2015 by
The Crowood Press Ltd
Ramsbury, Marlborough
Wiltshire SN8 2HR

www.crowood.com

British Library Cataloguing-in-Publication Data
A catalogue record for this book is available from the British Library.

ISBN 978 1 78500 033 1

Typeset by Jean Cussons Typesetting, Diss, Norfolk

Printed and bound in India by Replika Press Pvt Ltd

CONTENTS

INTRODUCTION

Blacksmithing is of one of the oldest crafts. People who want to develop these blacksmithing skills may come to it from a wide variety of other activities. You may already have the kit and want to do something less functional that allows you to express yourself creatively. You may be skilled in other creative crafts and want to expand your materials and skills repertoire to include blacksmithing. You may even have a project in mind and are intrigued by how forging is done. Rather than buying a ready-made product, or commissioning someone to make it for you, you may well become so fascinated that you want to do it yourself.

Unfortunately for would-be practitioners, blacksmithing is rather equipment-hungry. You will need something heavy and flat, preferably an anvil, upon which to hit the metal, and a hammer to hit it with. That is the way most smiths start out on their journey of exploration.

We will begin by learning about the anvil and using fire, especially managing the various techniques needed to control and manipulate the heat. Please note that the availability of fuel varies from place to place; this book refers to the use of coke, which is universally used in Britain, but coal and charcoal require different tech-niques.

In the course of time, as your knowledge, experience and skill accumulates, the need will arise for more and more tools. A selection of hammers for various tasks should be available for the smith's use. There are five types of tongs described in this book, and later, a chapter showing how to make your own tongs.

Almost uniquely in the world of making, smiths have the ability to make their own tools. Besides hammer and tongs, to perform any tasks except pure forge work, other tools must be available. These will be collected or made as progress demands. Hitherto, it has been assumed that the novice has had access to tools from 'elsewhere'. However, if there is more than a passing interest, the blacksmith will need some personal tools, which do not need borrowing. During working, having the right tool handy to help the flow of the job will enhance a sense of achievement, and reduce frustration. Besides which, there is a lot of satisfaction to be had from working with your own homemade tools.

Basic techniques, such as drawing down, bending, marking out and splitting, will be explained, and you will be able to practise these and more advanced processes while working on various projects involving the introduction of skills of growing difficulty. In the first few chapters all of the instruction is about traditional ironwork, and the tools with which it is made. These are the building blocks, necessary to lay down before you can express your creativity.

In Britain, until recently there was a very stuffy attitude towards ironwork. Architectural styles changed, but to a large extent, ironwork lagged behind. Smiths themselves were not encouraged to experiment, and the paragon work of Jean Tijou (active circa 1690–1710) continued to be held in high esteem. There were exceptions, obviously, and some really innovative work was done in the late nineteenth and early twentieth centuries. After the Art Deco period, however, ironwork declined, and was dropped from architectural studies. Some of the good work from those periods was quite organic, and in Chapter 6 we will demonstrate some of the techniques employed in its manufacture.

Whatever experience you bring to this book, and whatever you hope to achieve, it has been written for present-day craft explorers to enable everybody to unfold some of the mysteries of this fascinating, ancient craft.

GETTING STARTED

The anvil

The smith's most important piece of equipment is his anvil. In Britain, the most usual kind of anvil is the London Pattern. This shape evolved about 300 years ago, and has hardly been bettered. There are also Birmingham Pattern and Portsmouth Pattern anvils in use, as well as various other slightly different models.

Portsmouth Pattern; similar to Birmingham, but with extra squared-off beak at other end.

Birmingham Pattern anvil; similar to London, but missing the table.

OPPOSITE: **London Pattern anvil; the most popular shape used in Britain for 300 years. The height of the anvil should enable the smith to rest his hand upon the anvil while keeping the back straight.**

Parts of the anvil

The beak, also called the bick, beck, pike, horn and other names, is the prominent characteristic of the anvil. Because of its tapering shape, it has an infinite number of radii, used in creating curves.

The square hole at the other end, the heel,

of the anvil is called the hardie hole. It is so named after the cutting tool, which is the most frequently used anvil accessory. During a

Heel end of London anvil, showing hardie hole and pritchel hole.

Selection of tools for hardie and pritchel holes, where they can be seen.

lifetime of working, a smith will invent – and copy – innumerable square-shanked tools to be secured in that hole.

Beside the hardie hole, there is another, smaller, round hole called the punch hole, or pritchel hole. This is used to support flat material when punching through the metal; because of its malleability, the material around the hole would otherwise be forced down around the hole and need re-flattening.

The face of the anvil is hardened. Even though the metal is hot and soft when it is being hit, the face needs to be hard wearing. Until the nineteenth century, anvils were made of wrought iron, and the face, of hard steel, was fire-welded on. After time in use, the body of the anvil would slightly compress at the left, most-used part of the face, and it would hollow. Forged (wrought iron) anvils have holes under the beak and heel where the huge tongs were deployed in placing the anvil in and out of the fire during manufacture. Present day anvils are usually cast steel, and have no holes. They do not hollow so much.

The beak is usually placed at the left when the anvil is used by a right-handed person. At the opposite side of the face, at the left hand end, is a small radius. This is used for a variety of reasons, which will be explained as we progress.

Radius at left end of face.

Height of the anvil

For ergonomic reasons, it is fairly important to adjust the height of your anvil to your needs. You can end up with a sore back if it is too high or low. To assess the height, stand beside the anvil, with your arm hanging down beside you and place the palm of the hand straight out, it should rest gently on the face of the anvil. If your arm is bent, the anvil is too high, and if you have to bend your body, it is too low.

Stand

Many anvils are supplied with a cast iron stand. These are usually too low, because they are meant to be used in an industrial situation, where a striker hits the tools upon the metal

Other side of steel welded anvil stand, showing brackets for frequently-used tools.

Steel welded anvil stand, with retractable container for quenching pot in front of smith, and scroll iron in socket.

with a sledge-hammer. They also seem to increase the noise emitted by the anvil. In the traditional country smithy, the anvil was placed upon an elm trunk, which was sunk about two feet into the earth floor.

In a modern shop, where space is usually at a premium, a steel stand, which is movable, is convenient. Brackets for accessories and tools can be welded on to one of these stands, too.

FORGING SCALE

When you are forging, the hot metal oxidizes, shedding 'scale' (Fe_3O_4) on the anvil face. This scale is very hard, and can cause marks on the underside of the metal you are working. It is advisable to blow it off, or swipe it away, as you work.

The fire

Side blast and bottom blast

There are different kinds of fire – sometimes called a forge (but a forge can also refer to the building). The fire usually associated with rural and industrial use is the side blast, but the modern fire usually used abroad, and for the artist blacksmith, is the bottom blast.

The side blast has a tuyere (tue iron) through which the air is fed into the fire. It is made of either cast iron or mild steel, and has a double skin with water circulating inside. The water is fed from a bosh (tank) situated at the back of the fire and circulates by convection, to prevent the tue from overheating, which could cause it to burn. The danger in this is to forget to top up the water, and the tue burns out. This is a very

Water bosh at back of fire, with air regulating valve.

expensive omission. Obviously the water evaporates, more so when hot, so that it is essential to check the water level every morning before lighting, and more so when using the fire at a high temperature.

The bottom blast is fed with air through a tue in the base of the fire.

The side blast fire is usually on a table with the supply fan underneath. There are quiet fans, which run all day unobtrusively, although some of the older types of fan make a terrible noise.

The base of the fire is forge dust, one of the inert products of combustion. The fuel sits on the dust, and is raked into the fire as needed.

The air supply needs to be variable. There are different kinds of valves for this job. Some fans have a motor whose speed can be regulated by a rheostat. If it is a noisy motor, this is essential, but it does not matter much with a quiet fan. The fire must be able to change for different conditions.

Lighting the fire

Old coke is raked away from the tue, exposing some clinker from the previous working. Clinker is the silicon from the fuel, turned into a crude form of glass, which drips down through the fire and forms a lump. Having a very high coefficient of expansion, it hardens as it cools and cracks with a 'clink' and hence the name.

Throw the clinker away, and make a dish-shaped depression in the dust, about 100 deep and 150 across, in front of the tue (side blast) or above the tue (bottom blast). There is always plenty of dust created during working, so some must be discarded each time you light. (Note: throughout the book, unless otherwise stated, measurements are given in mm, but in blacksmithing the unit is customarily omitted.)

Kindling sticks, about 125 long, will be needed, and some old newspaper. Roll up three or four sheets of paper into a ball, and place in the hole. Spread about fifteen sticks around the paper like a wigwam, and switch on the blower. The valve should be almost closed. Light the paper, and introduce a breath of air, sufficient to blow the flame on the paper. Keep an eye on the sticks, and when they start to flame, rake some (preferably old) coke onto the sticks. Always leave a hole in the top of the pile of sticks, to let the smoke out, and it will shortly ignite as a flame. Build the coke around the sticks and it will slowly ignite, and the whole thing will be ready to use in about five minutes.

Fire cleaned out, ready for lighting, showing side blast tuyere, ball of paper and kindling sticks.

Conserving fuel

Fuel is expensive, so keep the blast down most of the time. Metal will heat in its own good time, and regulation is slowly learned. Students and other learners have huge fires, wasting fuel. The experienced smith will work with about a quarter of the size of fire. One of the perils of big fires is that the temperature inside is beyond the burning point of steel, and irretrievable damage is easily done. Students' scrap bins are full of burnt metal.

Watch the colour

It is best to keep withdrawing the metal from the fire constantly, to check the colour of the work. The progression of colours goes from black heat to maroon, to blood red, to bright red, to orange, to yellow, then white. Orange is the best colour to work with. Malleability changes radically through the colour range, and if you are trying to change the shape a lot, it needs to be orange.

The effectiveness of the hammer is dulled as the temperature drops. This is sometimes useful, because when, for instance, you are trying to impart a smooth finish to the work, blemishes can be removed with light blows at maroon heat.

Fire management

Fire management, or forge management, has many facets, and some people never get the hang of it. Observation is of prime importance. There are dangers, which should be known, and avoided. Apart from keeping yourself out of the fire, and avoiding picking up hot metal (which is easily done), you need to respect the dangers inherent in the coke.

Coke explosion
During coke manufacture, coal is heated in a sealed oven, to drive off volatiles such as gas, benzene, tar, pitch and others. What is left is almost pure carbon, which is ejected from the coke oven and quenched. The resulting smoke-less fuel is used by smiths as a convenient way of heating metal.

During the quenching, small amounts of water can be absorbed into orifices in the coke. If this is driven off slowly, at the side of the fire, that is fine; if, however, the coke is put directly on the fire, the water in these holes is heated fiercely and can explode with a loud bang, which is often accompanied by very hot pieces of coke flying at the smith. (Water expands 1,700 times when turning to steam.)

Carbon monoxide

When you look at a smithy fire you can see small, semi-luminous flames which have a bluish tinge. This is carbon monoxide (CO) – a deadly poison – burning off, to form carbon dioxide (CO_2), which, though not poisonous, does not support life. If you extinguish these bluish flames by putting wet coke on the top it allows the CO to escape into the atmosphere. This is dangerous. The coke should, therefore, be introduced at the edge of the fire, and drawn closer to the centre gradually, leaving the flames to burn off, to CO_2.

Leaving the fire safely

If you need to leave the fire during the day, get a piece of wood, about 150×100×50. Rake a large hole in the coke, and place the wood in it. Cover the wood with hot coke until it is completely submerged, and switch off the blower, and the wood will turn slowly to charcoal. You will be able to leave it for about an hour and a half. When you return, restart the

fan, and the fire will spring into action very quickly – a minute or so.

Equipment and tools

The rake

The rake should be the most-shiny piece of equipment in the forge. It sits on the fire, and is used each time the work is put into the fire.

The fire should be a shallow upturned cone shape, and should not be allowed to develop into a hollow. That is because the shallower the fire, the nearer to the clinker the work gets. Clinker adheres wonderfully to the metal, and although it is semi-liquid, it has a high density. This causes deep marks to be made on the surface if clinker remains during forging. Raking the surface of the metal after withdrawal from the fire should clean it off.

The rake should be held so that the blade is horizontal. The dust around the bowl of the fire will eventually consolidate, except for the

FIRE TOOLS

Apart from the rake, it is good to have a poker and a shovel (sometimes called a slice).

A good tip – especially when you are busy – is to have different handles on them, so you can glance down and pick the right one without having to look at the other end.

Fire tools, showing different ends, so the correct one can be seen at a glance, saving time when busy. Note how shiny they are, from frequent use.

immediate surface of the bowl. The fresh coke will lie on the dust and be drawn easily into the fire. If you turn the rake so that it is vertical, it will disturb the dust and draw it into the fire. Of course, the dust is inert and will impair the working of the fire.

Bench

It is advisable to have a bench, with vice attached. Because of the boisterous nature of working in the vice, the bench should be very sturdy: 50 or more thick for the top, and 75 square at least for the legs. The bench does not need to be very big; 1200×600 is enough, but the bigger the better. However, the more surface, the more clutter you can expect to collect upon it.

Vices

Leg vice
The best kind of vice for smithing is the leg vice. It is traditionally made of wrought iron, and therefore very tough. Hammering can be done on work in its jaws with impunity.

One drawback to the leg vice is that its jaws do not open parallel. The movable jaw is on a pivot about 300–450 below the jaw. This means that the work is held by the bottom edge of the jaw when it is open. Consequently, the work is not as secure as it would be with parallel jaws. It also means that the work can be marked by the jaw digging into the hot metal.

On new leg vices (rarely seen in smiths' shops) the jaws are grooved for extra grip. This marks hot metal badly. Erasing the grooves, or, if you have the time, drilling the jaws, and adding a plain mild steel jaw grip, with the screws countersunk out of the way, is time well-spent.

Engineer's vice
The other common vice is the engineer's vice. This has jaws that open parallel, and give a uniform grip. They usually have removable grips, well grooved. For smith work, replacing them with softer mild steel, plain grip jaws is a good move, as it saves marking the work.

Engineer's vices are usually cast, sometimes in iron, sometimes in steel. Cast iron is brittle, and the iron vice will not take hammering – they can split in two. Therefore, the engineer's vice should only be used for such activities as

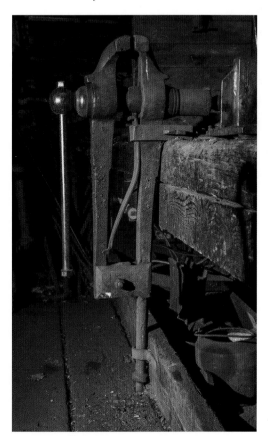

Leg vice; very strongly built, so it withstands heavy blows.

sawing, filing or grinding. The screws should be kept clean, and oiled about twice a year.

Hammers

There are many types of hammer, each designed for a particular job. I have met a tool collector with 435 different hammers, culled from many trades. He knew each one's use.

Hammers are made in various shapes, and each country seems to have its own variation. The ball peen (pane, pein, pien) hammer is known as the engineer's hammer in Britain. It seems to be only in Britain and the USA that this is 'the ordinary hammer'. Most other countries regard the ball peen as a specialist hammer, and their ordinary hammer is the cross peen hammer, taking local variations. The ball peen is useful for various operations, and particularly for hitting inside curves, where it will not mark the surface like a flat face. The cross peen will line up at the end of bars, for spreading metal outwards, for example fishtails. (Specialist hammers will be mentioned and described later.)

Tongs

Tongs are for gripping hot metal, and should be comfortable to hold, therefore they should fit the metal being forged. The possession of many pairs of different tongs, with jaws that fit different sizes of stock steel, makes working easier, so that the smith can concentrate on what is being hammered, instead of wrestling with uncomfortable tongs.

Ancillary tools

To perform any tasks except pure forge work, other tools must be available. A few of the essentials are: anvil fork, chisel, hot sett, rule, chalk and centre punch.

Materials

Mild steel

The most common material used in modern smithing is mild steel. This is the everyday steel, used in engineering for a great variety of purposes. To make it strong and durable, it contains about 0.25 per cent of carbon, and a small amount of manganese. It can be obtained from steel stockists in major towns, and is supplied in 6m lengths. Other types of steel used by smiths are tool steel and stainless steel.

Wrought iron

Many people talk of wrought iron as the generic term for shaped metal work. Strictly speaking, wrought iron is a kind of iron, which was formerly used for most purposes but was largely superseded by mild steel. It is available, but made from scrap and re-rolled for specialist, mainly conservation, use. It costs about ten times as much as mild steel. Malleability is its virtue, but it must be worked white-hot, otherwise it might de-laminate. Its ability to resist corrosion is higher than mild steel.

Pure iron

Another kind of iron – pure iron – is used for decorative work. This material contains no carbon or other elements, and is also quite soft. For non-load-bearing work, such as scrolls and leaf-work, it works beautifully in many processes, but is too soft for structural pieces. It can sag under its own weight. It also costs about ten times as much as steel.

Tool steel

There are many varieties of steel, some of which are collectively called tool steel. Hundreds of books on metallurgy detail the types of tool steel, and it can be a bewildering minefield for the beginner. Many experienced smiths do not know more than two or three types, and this can lead to problems when making tools for specific jobs, especially when using second-hand tool steel.

For the beginner, grade En 19 is a useful, and readily available grade of tool steel for general use, but if you need specialist jobs done, experts should be consulted. It is common to use the wrong grade, and for cracks to occur in tools. This is dangerous, as pieces can fly off at high speed and cause injury.

Most tool steel has a high (0.75 per cent+) carbon content, as well as a variety of added elements, which impart their own character-

FORGING TOOL STEEL

Generally speaking, the more carbon content, the harder the steel is to work. Other added elements will also make forging harder to accomplish.

istics to the finished steel. Some, including files, have higher amounts, up to 1.25 per cent carbon. The higher the carbon content, the more brittle the steel tends to be.

Half hard steel

Some jobs, for example making tongs, require steel that is not too hard, but harder than mild steel. A good supply of 0.5 per cent carbon steel is reinforcing bar, which can be found in scrap yards, or sometimes (with permission) at construction sites. This steel is not hardened after forging.

TEMPERING

Tool steel is heat treated to induce hardening. Heat treatment is a specialist subject, but usually involves heating the tool steel to a bright orange (we cannot measure these temperatures, but it is about 875°C) and quenching the part to be hardened. This makes it very hard, but brittle, and likely to break.

To make the metal less brittle, but still hard, it is heated again, gently, after the surface has been rubbed until it shines. During heating, the surface will colour with translucent oxides in the following sequence: pale straw, dark straw, purple, blue, grey.

This process is known as tempering. For most of our purposes, the tool steel is tempered to purple, which gives us a hard edge, resilient enough to stand up to hard work.

BASIC TECHNIQUES

Drawing down

Drawing down is the blacksmith's term for tapering, or reducing the size of material. Assuming now that you have got an anvil, a fire and a hammer, it is time to do some work.

A good preliminary exercise to practise both drawing down and bending is to make a rat tail handle. This is a task that involves drawing down the end of some 12 round steel along a distance of 150.

Cold practice

Take a 700 length of steel, making sure that the ends have any burrs removed. Take hold of the bar about a third of the way along. Stand about 300 away from the anvil, place the end of the bar at the far side of the anvil, and press the left hand, holding the steel, against the left leg, which is your 'third hand', keeping the steel steady on the anvil. Raise the left hand so that the bar is lifted, making the far end slope at about 15 degrees to the anvil. Holding the hammer at the end – do not 'choke' the hammer – raise the right hand until the

hammer face is about 15 degrees to the bar. This makes the hammer 30 degrees to the anvil. That will be the shape of the taper.

BURRS HURT

Safe working practices should be used always. Burrs on steel can cut hands.

Into the fire

Now, having tried all this cold, put the metal into the fire.

As a beginner, take a small hammer. You can do a lot of work with a small hammer. If you try to use a hammer that is too heavy, your arms will ache, and you can do permanent damage if you are not careful. Build up your strength gradually.

COLOUR CHECK

Until you have done quite a lot of practical forge-work, make a habit of drawing the metal out of the fire quite frequently, say, every thirty seconds, to check the colour. This is a necessary precaution. It is very easy to overheat the metal, and burn it beyond redemption.

OPPOSITE: **Rat tail handle.**

Starting the taper with a blunt point; body about 300 from anvil, left hand pressed against left thigh; steel bar at 15 degrees to anvil, hammer at 15 degrees to metal, making point 30 degrees. The taper is 25 long with rounded end about 3 wide.

When the metal has reached orange, place it on the far side of the anvil, just away from the edge, not overhanging. With the hammer at 30 degrees and the bar at 15 degrees, using mostly the wrist, hit the end of the bar four times. Turn it through a quarter turn quickly, and hit it again four times. Always draw down with the metal square. Keep hitting until the metal has turned maroon, and return to the fire. When the end of the bar is down to 3, stop. The taper should now be about 25 long.

Now is the time to elongate the taper. When the metal is orange hot again, place the bar on the beak with about 85 overhanging. Using all parts of the arm, hit the metal as hard as you can, drawing the metal every blow about 6

towards yourself. When you reach the end, turn again a quarter and repeat the procedure. After a couple of heats, the hitting will not need to be done at the part nearest you, so that a long taper will be achieved. Due to the use of the beak, the surface of the taper will be uneven, but that does not matter.

The next part takes place on the face of the anvil. Take another heat, and place the taper on the anvil. Hammer it until flat on all faces.

Hammer marks

If you find that the hammer is leaving marks all over the work, you are not holding the hammer at the right position. The height of the right hand needs to be such that the face of the

Continuing the taper. 85 over the beak, using all of arm to move hammer, spreading the metal
lengthways.

ANVIL MARKS

It is important to realize that in all of this hammering, the anvil makes marks on the underside when you hit the upper side. Not quite as prominent, but nevertheless significant.

hammer is flat on the work when it hits. Try to make the surface finish as smooth as possible.

Rounding off

To make the square section round, we need to take off the corners to make an octagon section. This should be carried out at orange heat. Take note that the thinner the material, the quicker it will heat up. This is where control of the valve on the fire is important. Also, the position of the metal in the fire determines how much heating it gets. The temperature gradient from the middle of the fire to the outside is very steep.

Next, at a lower temperature (maroon colour – you will not see the corners if it is orange) take off the corners of the octagon to make a hexa-decagon (16 sides). That is near enough to round, unless there are prominent projections which can be hit. When all of this is done,

THE ADDED VALUE OF TEXTURE

In former years, 'round' section meant round, and great lengths were taken to achieve this, in a smooth finish. Nowadays, we have 'texture' where the marks (facets) of manufacture contribute a pleasing finish to the work.

heat the end, draw it down square to 1.5, and round it off. It is important to make the end of the taper really fine, or it will look lumpy when finished.

Bending

Making the ring and wrapping the tail

Now we come to make the ring for the handle, giving practice in bending.

Centre punch hole, glowing brightly while surface of bar oxidizes to grey.

The inside diameter is about 35, so the length is about 150. At that distance from the start of the taper, mark the position of the start of the ring with a centre punch. Make a hole about 3 across. This will be seen when the metal comes out of the fire. The surface of the metal oxidizes to a grey scale when it cools, but inside the punch hole it will not oxidize.

Before placing the metal in the fire, bend it slightly towards the punched hole. This will not only show where to look for the hole, but it will

Bending metal towards centre punch hole, helping to locate it. The bend also serves to show where the bar should be placed in the fire.

Starting the bend for the ring. The hammer is the thickness of the metal away from the edge of the anvil, avoiding thinning the metal.

Turn the hammer so that it hits the metal against the side of the anvil, and does not make the metal go down the side of the anvil in a straight line. This must be the first part of the ring, and is quite sharply curved.

metal over the beak, where the beak is about 40 diameter. Knock the next part of the ring around the beak, hitting the cold end of the taper to use the leverage, until the cool part of the metal is reached.

Keep the ring at the same part of the beak. Remember that its diameter reduces. When the ring has reached past a right angle, place it under the beak, with the hot end upwards, so

dip nicely into the fire at the right point. After heating, slap the metal on the anvil to straighten it, and place the punched hole at the edge of the anvil at the radius at the left hand end. Take an English hammer with a ball-peen. Bring the ball-peen down on the metal, at a distance of the thickness of the metal away from the anvil. Hit it hard, and guide the hammer so that it hits immediately below the edge, and does not make the metal go in a straight line down the side of the anvil. It must be a curve. That is the beginning of the ring.

Now place the next part of the ring in the fire, with the completed part towards the edge where the temperature is lower. When there is enough heat place the already-curved

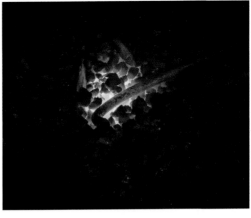

The next part of the ring in the fire, with the curved portion of the ring out of the side of the fire, keeping cool.

Continuing the ring over the beak, where the diameter is about 40. The metal should only be moved when it is hot, as it will kink if it is cold; reheat if necessary.

The finish of the ring, with tail at 60 degrees.

that the blows will be directed downwards (it is much easier to hit downwards). Continue until the ring is completed, and overlaps the stem until there is an angle of 60 degrees (that is, 8 o'clock).

Taking a pair of flat-bit tongs preferably with long handles and jaws, place them near a vice. Heat the tail material, place the ring in the vice, and pull the tail around the stem, making sure that the angle remains at 60 degrees. Finish by pressing the very end of the tail against the stem.

This ends the making of the rat's tail handle, which can be used for any number of implements, such as a poker, a shovel or a brush.

Wrapping the tail with the tongs, keeping the angle at 60 degrees. Care must be taken to see that the angle remains constant, as this affects the shape and appearance of the final tail.

Flat bit tongs, preferably with long jaws.

Useful tools for bending

Anvil fork

The anvil fork is such a simple tool but so useful. Bends can be made accurately, and incorrect bends can be remade easily with the fork. A series of forks with different width prongs are an asset. There will be many references to the use of forks later.

Examples of rat tails; in this case, a companion set made with rat tail handles.

Anvil fork.

Scroll wrench

To enhance the use and precision of forks, a scroll wrench can be employed. This will pinpoint the position of the bend, while keeping metal beyond the bend in a straight line. A selection of widths between the prongs, using several scroll wrenches, will increase the versatility of the user.

Scroll wrench, used with fork to bend exactly where required.

Bending flat steel in the vice, using a heavy piece of steel to smooth the finish.

a heavy piece of flat steel on the surface of the bend before hammering. Further, the jaws of the vice can cause galls on the underside; this can be offset by adding a soft plate over the edge of the jaw of the vice.

Bending like this should not be done with an engineer's vice, except for small, light sections of steel.

Jigs

When there are several identical bends to be made, a jig should be formed, around which the bend should be made quickly and accurately. A jig is a tool which usually has only one use. Pieces of scrap plate and odd lengths of scrap bar can be used to form a jig.

Keeping a sharp bend

Occasionally, a sharp bend needs to be made. In this case, the exact position of the bend should be marked by a centre punch dot, at least 3 across, so that it can be seen when it emerges from the fire. A can of water should be at hand, and the metal on each side of the bend should be cooled within 12 of the dot. The bend should then be made, either in the vice or in the forks. Some practice is advisable. Care should be taken applying the water, because steam causes scalds.

Vice

The vice can also be used for bending, where a long straight bend needs to be made in a piece of thin steel. However, take care: using the vice can lead to uneven surfaces caused by hammer marks, so to achieve a smoother finish, place

Examples of jigs for bending.

Marking out
and splitting

Initial marking out is done with chalk. Engineer's chalk, sometimes referred to as French chalk and sometimes as soapstone, is used for this purpose. It is a hard substance which will take a sharp edge, essential for accuracy, when needed. If, however, the metal is to be heated, the quickly oxidizing surface will shed the chalk, so more permanent marks are necessary, either by centre punching or marking with a cold chisel.

For an example of marking out and splitting, the back plate of a hanging basket bracket is a good one.

Engineer's chalk, sharpened for clear marking.

MAKING A BRACKET PLATE

Marking out

The material is 50 × 6 × 325 long. With the edge of the chalk finely sharpened with an old file, mark the length of the cut to be made – 75 – from each end. Then carefully measure the exact centre of the bar, twice; once near the end of the bar, and once near the 75 mark, and make a small mark at each one. Check they are accurate, and join up using a rule. The next job is to mark this line deeper.

Cold cutting

A cold chisel is for cutting and marking cold metal: a hot chisel, or hot sett, is used for cutting hot metal. Here we are using a cold chisel.

Stand at the heel end of the anvil, away from the beak. Position the plate on the face of the anvil, with the chalk mark you wish to cut nearest you. Place the end of the blade of the chisel at the end of the chalk line. Make sure that the end of the chisel blade nearest you is exactly in line with the chalk mark. The chisel should be sloping away from you, about 10 degrees. Hit the chisel, which will make a triangular mark. Then bring the chisel to vertical, exactly on the line, and hit it again. That is the start of the cut.

Because it is difficult to see the chalk line, which is partly hidden by the chisel, it is not easy to put the chisel exactly in line with the first mark. To make the cut line continuous, place the chisel $^1/_3$ of the way into the existing line, align it with the chalk line, and hit again. That should ensure continuity. Repeat until the line reaches the end. By doing this stage cold, time can be spent, and there will be no danger of burning yourself.

Cold chisel placed on chalk mark to start groove. By working cold, you can take care to ensure accuracy and evenness.

Hot splitting

Now we put it in the fire. To do this job, box tongs will be needed to hold the flat plate. The cheeks on the jaw will prevent the plate from slipping sideways out of the tongs. Position the plate flat in the fire. Do not have the fire burning fiercely for this job. It is easy to burn the metal. The mark from the cold chisel will indicate exactly where the hot sett is to be placed, and will speed up the process. When the plate is orange, remove it from the fire, and brush the surface. Turn it quickly on its side, and knock it on the side of the fire to dislodge any dust which has gathered in the groove, and prevent it from bouncing up into your face; it hurts!

Box tongs holding flat bar. Note the cheeks, which hold the metal tightly and prevent the sideways movement and possible escape, when the bar is hit on the edge.

Quickly put the plate on the face of the anvil, with the cut nearest you, and stand at the end of the anvil as before. Place the hot sett into the end of the groove and hit it. Move the hot sett towards you, as with the chisel. Start again at the far end, and do it again. The anvil will suck the heat out of the plate very quickly, and it will need reheating soon. Do not forget to remove dust and scale from the plate each time it is withdrawn.

Cutting with hot sett. Note offset blade, enabling rear (closest) edge to be seen and accurately placed by the user.

Using thin plate before sett cuts right through, to prevent damage to sett blade.

When the cut is nearly through, put a small piece of 3 thick steel under the plate. When the sett does break through, this will stop the blade blunting itself on the hard anvil. Forging and finishing the flat scrolls will be described later.

FASTENINGS

There are many ways of attaching metal pieces to each other, without using an electric welder. The traditional ways are invariably more attractive looking, as well as being effective. Some of the commonest methods, described here, are rivets, collars and tenons.

Rivets

These are like little nails, and have several kinds of heads. The commonest is the round head, which looks like a small mushroom. It is necessary to drill holes in both pieces of work, where they touch. The tail of the rivet is pushed through both pieces, and the tail is hammered to make another head, fastening them together.

If there is more than one fastening to make, one of the items will be drilled at each point where the two components touch, and the other component will have only one hole made. After the first rivet is hammered, the drill will be sent through the other holes in turn, and the rivets will line up. However, trying to drill all of the holes first will inevitably result in some of them being out of line.

The rivet head is supported by a dolly, a matching piece which has a rivet-shaped depression in it into which the rivet fits. The tail can either be hammered flat, or it can be made into another head by using a snap, which is the same as a dolly but goes on top. In this case, the amount of tail left protruding must be 1½ times the diameter of the rivet, which gives the right quantity of material to make a head. Where another head might be in the way, another way to head the rivet is to countersink the place where the head is to be, and fill the countersunk hole with the tail. This can then be filed, if necessary. Where protrusions are inconvenient or unsightly, some rivets have countersunk heads.

There are also pan heads, which are like truncated cones, or cheese heads, which are squat cylinders.

Collars

Collars are small sections of steel wrapped around two or more components to fasten them together.

To make a collar, careful measurements must be taken where the two pieces meet. A mandrel must then be made, around which the collar is formed. The mandrel is made from a bar of the same material as those to be attached. It should be bent back upon itself, and tapered down to just over half of the full size. At the point on

OPPOSITE: **Round head rivet.**

Example of simple collar, holding together two scrolls in a decorative way.

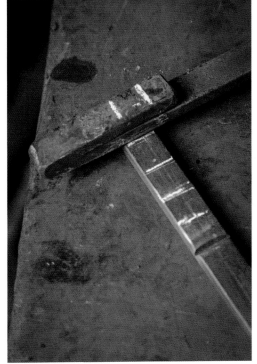

Marking length of collar, using mandrel.

the mandrel where the thickness is the same as the joint to be made, a chalk mark is made around the mandrel. A short piece of steel, the section of the collar, is placed on the anvil, and the length of the collar is marked as follows: place the chalk-marked part of the mandrel at the end of the collar bar, and turn it through 90 degrees three times; chalk the bar, and add two times the thickness of the bar. That will give the length of material for the collar.

At this point, cut into the surface, halfway through, with a hot sett. Put this short length into the fire, and heat until orange. Bring it out and bend it back on itself, to make a U-shape. The U should be the same width as the metal to be fixed. Make sure that the legs of the U are exactly the same. Put the mandrel into the U and knock the legs over the mandrel. Square

Making the U for the collar.

hammer the legs over the mandrel. There will be a gap. Hammer the sides, base and top of the collar into a rectangular form, and the gap will close. It is now knocked off the mandrel. It will have round corners. Some people leave the corners round, and some square them off.

The collar should then be heated, opened out with the bow pliers, and applied to the joint. This must be done at speed, as the collar will cool quickly and not move into place. Some support will be necessary underneath the collar to get it to close up.

the U, and bring the legs parallel. Reheat, and bend the free leg over the mandrel.

At this point, detach the U from the bar. The U can then be placed carefully in the fire, using the bow pliers. Be careful – it is easy to lose it in the fire. Draw the collar out of the fire, place it upon the mandrel at the chalk mark, and

Tenons

Tenons, with mortises, are usually used in framework, such as gates. The simplest tenoned joint is for balusters, where the hole is punched in the rail, and the baluster is swaged.

Stages of collar.

USING A SWAGE

A swage is a tool made from two solid pieces of tool steel, hinged together with a handle made from either round section or flat section substantial steel, with a ring at the end, forming a spring, which keeps the two parts of the swage together. The simplest swage converts a square cross section into a round one. The two halves of the swage have semicircular grooves running along the centre, which squash the hot metal into their shape, forming a round bar.

When the tenon is carefully marked off, forming a shoulder, the tenon has a definite support. A limited amount of tenon will protrude through the rail, and this is riveted over.

ABOVE: **Swage, usually hit by a sledge hammer, makes round sections; here shown with the tenon.**

LEFT: **Tenon, showing shoulder; also shown is the bar, with the tenon marked at the end before forging. The swage does not make a clean job of the shoulder, so the waste must be either filed off or dressed with a monkey tool.**

Tenon through rail. The length of the tenon determines the size of the head to be produced.

Tenon riveted. The hammer is inclined slightly to form a dome on the rivet head.

Heels

Heels are made on the end of bars, which are part of a structure that has to maintain rigidity. They are to be found on most traditional gates. A simple heeled joint would have been used in making a bracket protruding from a wall. (The making of heels and mortise and tenon joints is explained towards the end of the making of a hanging basket bracket; *see* Chapter 7.)

In forming frames for gates and other large structures, the tenons are specialized. To increase the surface area of the end of the rail, to enhance structural rigidity, the end of the rail bar is left long and is upset to create a large lump on the end. This is then formed into a heel, from which a tenon is forged as well. This tenon is elongated, and enters a long mortise, which has rounded ends. The tenon is then heated, and formed into a long rivet head.

Upsetting is very time and energy consuming (*see* Chapter 5). Rather than upsetting, on inspection of old gates which have been shot blasted, it can be seen that there is a weld, about 100 from the heel, which suggests that the heels were made separately, from large pieces of iron, and hammered down with sledge hammers. These large pieces would have been much easier to place in and out of the fire, rather than manipulating huge bottom rails.

Punching tools for tenons

Historically, punching holes preceded drilling, and is still used for several reasons. A punched hole is stronger than a drilled one, because there is very little metal lost: it all goes sideways. There is a slight swelling around a punched hole for that reason, and it is aesthetically pleasing. Punched holes can be any shape you like.

Punches are in various forms. The hand-held punch is usually made from 16 octagon or hexagon tool steel, and is 250–300 long. It is this long because the holding hand is further away from the hot metal to be punched. The working end of the punch should be about 6 across. If it is any smaller, it will heat too much while in contact with the metal, and soften. It is possible to upset the end inside a hole, and ruin everything by riveting the two together. If the end of the punch is larger than 6 it will be more difficult to force it through the hot metal.

The hand punch, being so long, needs the hammer to be lifted higher than usual, and gives the possibility of hitting the hand with the hammer. Using a shorter punch with a rodded handle is more convenient, but making the punch takes a little longer. (Making the rodded handle will be described later, in Chapter 4.)

Attaching mortises and tenons by riveting

Make sure that the tenon's back face is perpendicular to the shaft of the bar, and that there are no gaps anywhere between the heel and the plate. The amount of tenon protruding through the hole should be one and a half times the diameter of the tenon. Check this while it is cold.

During riveting, the bar will have to be held in a vice. Check that the vice does not have any serrations that can make marks on the bar. If it does, you will need to have some vice grips of smooth, thin metal, either copper or mild steel.

Have everything to hand at the vice before heating the tenon to bright orange. Place the bar with the tenon about 12 from the jaws,

GAS ALTERNATIVE

If you have gas available, Oxy-acetylene or Oxy-propane, heating the tenon can be much more controlled, and reheats can be done easily. This is a luxury however.

check that the back plate is the right way round, put it in position over the tenon, and hit the tenon hard and quickly, flattening out the head of the rivet. Finish it with the ball peen to round it off.

MAKING YOUR OWN TOOLS

In this chapter we will make a number of small tools, which will be useful as well as providing a grounding in the basic processes, as you try your hand at these: round hand punch, cold chisel, rodded punch, drift, anvil fork, scroll wrenches, hot sett and fuller.

Hand punch

Hand punches are used for making and enlarging holes. When making the hanging basket bracket, for example, you will punch the hole with a square punch. It is useful to have some punches of different sections and widths to hand.

The round punch is a good example to start with.

Taking a length of tool steel (for example, grade En19 about 250–300 long and about 16–20 octagon section) and heat the end in the fire, until orange.

Having heated the end to orange, hit it on one side of the octagon near the edge of the anvil. The bar should be held at a shallow slope – about 5 degrees – to create a 10-degree taper. The end should be forged square, down to about 6 across. The corners should now be drawn down, and then removed.

To make the taper very smooth, so that it does not drag on the inside of the hole when enlarging, the marks should be taken off. This final finish is imparted when the metal is maroon colour, because the hammer makes less of an impression when the metal is cooler. The left hand revolves the bar very slowly while the hammer hits the surface perfectly flat, making a smooth finish. This will take some time, but it is worth it. A shine can be achieved with patience. Reheating will have to be done, but take care not to overheat, as larger marks will be made.

When this is finished, grind the end flat. Chamfer, by grinding, the top where the punch is to be hit, and during use keep this chamfer intact, for safety.

WORKING TOOL STEEL

The forging temperature for tool steel is a narrow range, from orange down to red. Above orange, the special ingredients of the steel might deteriorate, and below red, the steel becomes too hard to work. Working tool steel is more arduous than mild steel. A useful analogy compares 'butter in the fridge, with butter on the table'.

OPPOSITE: **Chamfered finish to chisel.**

Cold chisel

As the cold chisel is one of the most frequently used tools, it is useful to know how to make one. Tools such as chisels can often be found at sales, usually in dreadful condition, but they can easily be refurbished, and made into special tools cheaply. Chisels wear out, too, so this procedure is the same for refurbishing chisels.

Take a piece of tool steel, 22 octagon by about 150 long. It is useful to have a pair of hollow bit tongs which fit snugly around the tool steel. Heat one end to orange.

Place the heated end near the far edge of the anvil, as for the punch, but this time raise the left hand to make a slightly shallower taper,

REMOVING THE MUSHROOM

Old chisels tend to have 'mushrooms' on the heads. These mushrooms should be removed by grinding off, and a chamfered finish made. If a chisel with a mushroom is hit, and resistance disappears, the chisel shoots through the hand, taking some of the hand around the base of the thumb with it. Apart from the pain, this is dangerous, and stops the sufferer from working.

Maintenance of tools is important.

USE OF THE FLATTER

The surface of the blade of the chisel should be perfectly flat. If your hammering is not up to scratch, it might have left hammer marks on. A way to flatten the surface is to use a flatter. This is hit with a sledge hammer, and produces a perfectly flat surface.

Flatter in use with sledge hammer.

The sledge hammer, or forehammer, comes in different weights, but the most common is the 7lb (approximately 3kg). It has a longer shaft than a hand hammer, which requires two hands to operate it. The sledge is an extended version of the hand hammer so to hold it, take the end of the shaft in the right hand, and hold the shaft about 250 from the head with the left hand. The right hand guides the progress of the head, and the left is for lifting.

Practice is needed, and much care must be exercised, in using a sledge. The hard head can, if hit upon the anvil with force, shatter, causing injury. It is important to be able to stop the head if something goes wrong. Time spent in practice is time well spent. The sledge can hasten the work considerably.

about 15 degrees. As you flatten the bar, keep it directly in line with the flat of the octagon, and occasionally turn it through 90 degrees and keep the sides parallel. Draw the taper down until the end is less than 3 thick. The end of the bar will round, and the very end will look like a pair of lips. This is because the end has not been made into a blunt point. It needs cutting off at right angles to the axis.

Sharpening the chisel

The edge should now be ground on the grindstone. The finished edge should be 80 degrees. Sometimes the very corners are taken off, but not always. The edge is put on before hardening, because grinding can overheat the metal and 'draw the temper'.

HARDENING AND TEMPERING

This is an important process to master, as it is used for many tools and determines to some extent the length of time between sharpening of tools.

Take the sharpened chisel is placed in the fire, and the end brought up to bright orange over a length of about 40, taking care not to overheat.

Have a source of water handy, for quenching. Put the last 20 into the water, cooling it out completely. Rub the surface with an old file, or stone, until the surface is shiny bright metal. Do this quickly.

Look at the surface, which will start to colour in the following sequence: white, pale straw, dark straw, purple, blue, grey. The heat in the metal behind the quenched part will conduct into the quenched portion, making the colours on the surface. The colours indicate the inner temperature.

How it works

The metallurgical details can be researched, but suffice it to say that the quenching from bright orange hardens the steel to such an extent that it becomes brittle and will break. By tempering – raising the temperature slightly – some of this brittleness is relieved, and the steel becomes tough. The colour purple is the correct one for a chisel.

Testing

After tempering, the edge of the chisel should always be tested. It is no good trying out tools after heat treatment and finding that they shatter, crack, or become blunt, especially if they are going for somebody else's use.

Take a piece of scrap 20 round bar, about 150 long, and place it on the table of the anvil, where it will not roll away. Put the centre of the hardened edge on the round bar, and hit the upper end sharply.

If the hardening is correct, it will make a mark about 1.5 deep across the bar. The edge of the chisel will be polished in an arc, where it has bitten into the bar. Now test the corners. The sharpened edge should not have changed its shape at all. Now it is available for use.

If, however, the edge cracks, or is depressed, the sharpening, hardening and tempering must take place again, with greater care observed in achieving the correct colour.

Rodded punch

The rodded punch is used for making holes in wooden-handled tools.

The next tool to be made after this rodded punch will be a hot sett, using the same cross section of tool steel, which we will now forge, using a sledge hammer and working with a striker.

Take a piece of En19 about 25 square, 160 long. Make sure that the tongs fit the section snugly. Remember that the forging temperature range is narrow, so beware of overheating. Have ready a sledge, a fuller and a flatter. The anvil should be low for this.

The smith brings the heated end of the tool steel out of the fire, and places it 25 over the edge of the anvil, placing the fuller on the top of the tool steel. The striker hits the fuller, making

Anvil lowered onto a smaller stand when using sledge hammer with a striker. This gives the hammer room to swing down onto flatter.

a groove in the top. (The example shown is a one-man operation, in case there's no striker. It demonstrates the shape of the taper (49). This will take longer than a two-man job.) The fuller is moved slightly away from the smith, and hit again. This is repeated until the end is reached. The steel will probably have cooled, so it's reheated. When the steel is brought out again, it's put on the anvil the other way up, and the process is repeated. Because of the hardness of the steel, progress will be slow. The sides of the steel will also swell out. The intention is to make the section at the beginning of the taper 22 × 16, ending as 16 × 8. The process needs to be done in the other plane. When the sizes are roughly correct, finishing will be done by the flatter.

Next, the corners must be removed, as there should be no corners inside a hole; corners

Punch tapered over anvil.

WORKING WITH A STRIKER

Because of the hard nature of tool steel, even when hot, it is easier to work it quickly by having two people working together. This was always the traditional system of working. The smith would have either a striker or an apprentice with him, and call upon the assistant when he needed help.

Remember the ergonomics of the anvil: the face should usually be level with the outstretched palm. When using a sledge, however, the height changes. Because there is now the metal, and above it a tool to be struck by the hammer, the anvil should be set lower. A good guide is to stand by the anvil with the hand straight down. The fingertips should rest upon the anvil face.

create stresses, leading to cracks. The tapered punch is placed on the anvil with the corners upwards, and struck with the flatter, rounding off to finish. This will raise the corners, making a hollow down the taper. These must be flattened out, leaving nothing concave on the taper. The end of the taper, which will have become convex, should be ground flat.

The rodded handle

Rodded handles are used extensively by smiths. Rods do not transmit shock as much as a wooden handle, and the handle can be used to hang them up, saving space and 'giving them a home to go to'.

Another fuller, this time a smaller one, about 6 across, will be needed for this part of the tool. The head of the punch will be about 35 long, and the rods have to be approximately halfway along. The whole of the punch should now be heated, taking care not to overheat the taper, which, because it is smaller, will tend to heat more quickly. Do not have the fire too lively.

Place the bar with corners up, and hit the corners, to make a chamfer about 3 wide on each one. Now place the 6 fuller on a corner, and make a groove. Make another right next to it, with no space in between. Turn the bar to the next corner, and groove it in line with the first grooves. Repeat on all corners. The rods will go into these grooves, and stay in place.

Now cut the punch off the stock metal (leaving about 80 to make the next project, the hot sett).

Sledge hammer or forehammer: The example shown is a one-man operation, in case there is no striker. It demonstrates the shape of the taper. (This will take longer than a two-man job.)

Gripping the taper, heat the head, and make a slight taper at the top. Make sure that the top of the head is ground smooth.

Take a length of 6 round rod, about 550 long. Mark the centre, and heat. Bend it right back in a loop, making sure that the ends are the same. The distance between the two rods should be slightly wider than the head of the punch. Place the head of the punch in a vice, leaving the grooves above the jaws of the vice. It should be at the end of the jaws, with the axis of the punch parallel with the jaws. Now take a long heat, at least 125 long; you might have to juggle the metal forward and back through the fire to achieve this. Have a pair of flat bit tongs to hand, next to the vice, and a small hammer. There is no time to waste, as the rods cool down quickly.

Take the rods out of the fire, and place over the head of the punch, with your hands away from you; quickly cross the rods and bring them

Taper at the top of punch, before grinding the top smooth. Note the grooves for the rodded handle.

as tightly as possible round the head. Do not cross them outwards, as they need to be twisted while parallel. Make sure that the rod is lined up with the grooves. To get them together, tap

Adding handle to punch.

Bringing rods together with hammer.

with the hammer, keeping the rods together at the end with the left hand. Now take the tongs, and grip the two rods about 12 away from the head, twisting them together, one complete turn, keeping the other end in order with the left hand. It is very important to do this whole operation quickly, as it is difficult to finish a half-twisted pair of rods. The twist will tighten the rods around the punch, and further prevent the rods slipping off.

Remove from the vice, and quench. If there is a discrepancy in the lengths of the rods, saw the longer one off.

Twisting handle to tighten rods.

Make sure that the ends of the rods are together, and place in the fire. Take a welding heat, and gently weld the ends together, carefully rounding off the end so that it is comfortable to use. Now take a longer, cooler heat, slightly away from the end of the rods and grip the last 75 in the vice. Taking a grip with the flat bit tongs, about 20 away from the jaws, twist the rods again, through one turn. You must turn the punch while twisting the rods, as the rods do not want to turn with the rest. Make sure it is all in line.

Welded punch handle.

Now make the handle, which also acts as a hook to hang it up. Heat the end of the rods, including the twist and the weld. Grip the weld carefully in the vice (so as not to stress it during the next move) and prise the two rods apart.

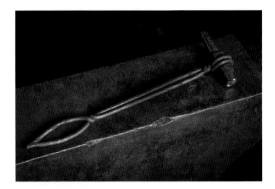

Completed punch handle.

The drift

A drift is a punch with both ends tapered. One taper is quite long with a gradual taper, and the other end is a short abrupt taper. This is used to finish the inside of holes. Therefore it must have a very smooth surface. This particular drift is for making the holes for wooden handles on smiths' tools.

We start with a piece of En19 tool steel, 25 × 16 × 100 long. It needs a taper, made from 25 long at one end, and another from 12 long at the other end. These tapers can be made with the sledge, and carefully smoothed with the flatter. The small end of each taper should be 20 × 10, no smaller. This will elongate the taper quite a lot. The corners should then be

Drift with first tapers.

Finished drift, showing very smooth surface, ensuring easy passage through holes.

hammered in to make a radius of 3 all along the drift. During the creation of the corners, a hollow will appear on the faces, which should be removed. Care should be taken to make sure that these corner radii are very smooth and even. This will ensure that progress through the hole is made easy. The ends of the drift should then be ground flat.

As the drift will be in contact with very hot steel during its use, there is no point in hardening, because the temper will be drawn as it gets hot. The purpose of the short taper is to facili-

tate the easy removal of the drift from the hole. The hammer will hit this end, and, because it is not hardened, it will mushroom slightly each time it is used. (The mushrooms should be ground off before the drift is put away.)

HOLES FOR SHAFTS

Parallel hole

Hot setts, fullers and some other tools have parallel holes – that is, not tapered – so that the shaft can be removed if necessary. Hot setts need to be heated to draw out the blade from time to time, as they are ground back for sharpening.

Tapered hole

Hammers, on the other hand, have tapered holes, so that the shaft can be wedged to stop it from coming off during use. If making a hammer, the drift should be partially driven in from each side, making a waist in the middle of the hole.

Drift being sent through hot sett at completion. Only when everything else has been done is the drift used.

Anvil fork

When bars need to be bent, a pair of forks is a useful tool. A set of forks, varying in width, will eventually need to be made, for versatility, so here is how.

Take a handling length of 20 round bar, heat the last 100 and bend it round, back upon itself. Find another, square piece of bar the required width of the forks, and place between the sides of the bent bar. Now hit the top prong until it sits flat on the spacer. Trim off the fork, and round the edges.

Make a piece of steel to fit the hardie hole. It should be a good fit, not too tight so that it cannot come out, but not loose and shaking about, either. Take the corners off this stem, and put a slight taper on it, too. Then weld on the fork. Such a simple tool, but so useful.

Anvil fork during making, showing gauge for parallel sides.

Scroll wrenches

Scroll wrenches can be made from mild steel rods, welded on to square bars. This method is quick, but they will inevitably bend out of shape. It is worth spending some time on making at least one pair of hard scroll wrenches.

Lorry (truck) springs work well as they are the right size. The material is so hard in its annealed (soft) state that they do not need hardening. And they will take any force you wish to give them. Scrap springs can be found at scrap yards. If you buy a whole spring, be extra careful when dismantling. Place the assembled spring in a vice before taking straps off, and let the vice out gently when the straps have gone, because they can be dangerous.

Take a leaf of the spring, and heat it until red. You will only be able to heat a small section at a time, but straighten out the curve as you go. This will anneal the spring.

Wire brush the surface, and draw the finished scroll wrench in chalk upon the face of the spring. It is essential that the prongs of the wrench are parallel. The cuts can be made by flame cutting (best done by an expert) or by using an angle grinder with a thin disc. If the latter, cut in gradually, at an angle, to remove the middle part. Finish the shaft with a normal grinding disc.

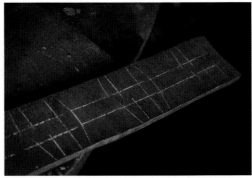

Scroll wrench marked out on lorry spring, using chalk.

Now the difficult part. The sides of the prongs should be ground into a round shape, carefully leaving the centres parallel. The outer sides of the prongs should be tapered towards the shaft of the wrench.

The shaft is completed by the addition of a piece of tube. Take off the sharp edges of the spring part of the shaft, and taper the end slightly.

Waste metal being removed from scroll wrench blank.

Preparation of scroll wrench blank for addition of handle.

Grinding round sides on scroll wrench prongs.

HANDLE HINTS

Permanent handle

To stop the handle coming off, make a groove in one side of the shaft. Make a note of the distance. Warm the tube, and hammer it on the shaft. With a narrow fuller, or a piece of wire, knock the tube down into the groove, and the handle will never come off.

Nut for gripping

Another tip is to weld a nut into the end of the handle. Sometimes parts with threaded ends have to be heated to repair or remake them. If you grip the threads, they become damaged and will not fit back in place. If they are gripped in your scroll wrench, the threads come out perfect.

Nut, welded into handle, and used to hold screwed parts when forging in fire. This preserves threads, which could be damaged by holding with tongs.

When you are established as a smith, and doing different types of job, you will find that it is necessary to have several widths of scroll wrench, capable of dealing with varying sections of metal.

one side, the punch needs to be repositioned, centrally, then it is hit again. Proceed through the bar. It will not go very far with each blow. Quench the punch after every three or four blows.

The bar will need reheating frequently, as the anvil takes the heat out of it.

Hot sett

The hot sett, or hot chisel, is a very useful tool. It has many applications in its different forms, for cutting and shaping metal. The piece of En19 left from making the punch, roughly 80×25 square, is an ideal size for a hot sett.

This is another job for a smith and striker. With the anvil set low, heat the bar and place it upon the anvil. The smith positions the punch centrally on one face, and the striker hits the punch, once. It is essential to check the position of the hole before striking again. If it is off to

LUBRICATING WITH COAL

When the punch has reached about 6 through, put a small piece of coal, about the size of a pea, into the hole. This will spread over the sides of the hole, forming a lubricant, making progress through the hole, and releasing, easier. When making deeper holes, the coal will blow the punch out of the hole.

As the punch nears the anvil, it will make a slightly different noise. Retrieve the punch, quench, and turn the blank over. It will have bent, and the sides will have thinned due to the effect of the punch. The striker should gently flatten the bar, before reheating.

At this point, check the shape of the metal around the hole. If you are accurate, it should be symmetrical, but if not, there is another trick. After heating, position the bar with the thin side of the hole down, over the bosh (trough), and pour water on the side of the hole. Quickly replace on the anvil, insert the punch, and hit. The hot side will expand, leaving the cold side the same, making the sides symmetrical.

Hot sett, spreading the sides of the hole sideways to elongate the hole, giving a better grip on shaft. The punch is driven into the hole, and the sides of the hole are spread out over the punch; then the punch is released, and driven in from the other side, and the process is repeated.

Symmetrical hole through hot sett.

Now is the time to regularize the hole. Heat the bar, place the punch into the hole, and hit the metal at the side of the hole with the sledge. It will expand sideways. Turn it over and repeat. The longer the eye of the punch, the better the grip on the wooden shaft. If it 'bellies' out, like the English engineer's hammer, then it is better still.

Sides of hot sett elongated before forging head and blade.

Forming the head of the sett

The head should be slightly tapered from the eye out. Grip one end of the bar after heating. Hit the end of the bar, forming the taper on all four sides. A flatter will make a more professional job. Finish by taking a wedge-shaped chamfer off each corner. This will produce a slight swelling at each corner, which can be ground off.

Hot sett, showing finished forged head, with swellings to be ground off.

Forming the blade

As mentioned earlier, having an offset blade not only moves your hand away from the hot metal, it enables the user to see the 'back end' of the blade. It is advisable to cut towards the smith, allowing the user to see that the blade follows the correct path.

Heat the bar, and insert the punch again. It will have to be hit into place. Place the blade end of the bar upon the beak, with the hole horizontal, and incline the hole 30 degrees to the right. (For a left-handed hot sett, incline 30° to the left.) Now hit the bar, flattening out the blade. This might take several heats. The blade will spread sideways, so with each heat bring it back onto the face of the anvil and narrow it back to parallel. The end will spread out into a semicircle, but take no notice. When the end of the blade has become 3 thick, then it is ready. Smooth the faces of the blade, and cut off the semicircle with the hardie.

Hot sett, forging blade over beak with 30 degrees offset. A round faced hammer is better for this job, as it avoids leaving marks on the upper part of the blade.

Correcting distortion

In all probability, the hole will have distorted. Now is the time to use the drift. The hole, after heating, should be placed over the hardie hole, and the drift knocked through. It might need several heats. Be careful not to distort the sides of the hole by flattening against the sides of the hardie hole. Check for straightness, and when correct, grind off the projections on the head. The blade should then be sharpened, not only across the end, but also up the sides. The blade can then be hardened.

Hot sett sharpened up the sides of the blade, to make V cuts.

Curved sett variations

Hot setts can be curved, and are used as such for shaping outlines, as well as cutting out parts for decoration. To make the curvature, while orange hot the blade should be pressed into a swage. As time goes by, and uses are found for curved setts, there never seem to be enough variations.

Hot sett sharpened from one side.

Hot setts seem to be used less in Britain than abroad.

Apart from the usual sharpening, there are occasions when the blade needs to be sharpened from one side. The sett can be used to create a chamfer around a flat shape, such as a door handle plate, with different radii and opposite sharpening.

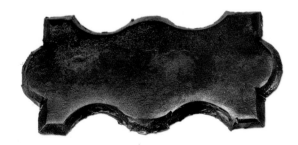

Chamfers made by one-sided hot setts on door handle plate, shown as cut by three curved setts and one straight sett. This example is shown before being filed smooth.

Fuller

The fuller is another tool which can be used not only for making items but also for decoration. As mentioned, fullers are used for necking down sections of metal. The radius produced by the fuller is quite pleasing to the eye, and in engineering terms, it is conducive to relieving stresses. A set of fullers is, therefore, a useful addition to your tool kit. They do not take much time to make, but they can facilitate better work.

Fullers, made with different end radii and curved ends.

Using a piece of En19 tool steel, the same size as for the hot sett, make the hole for a wooden handle as before. Make the head, and draw down the blade of the fuller to the breadth required. The end should be ground smooth, and the sharp ends of the blade should be relieved, to stop galling.

Fullers, too, can be curved. They can be used for creating curved grooves.

In Eastern Europe, hot setts and fullers are used in combination with side setts to make surface decoration, such as a plate or door knocker.

Eastern European surface decoration; made by the author, using thirty-two different setts and fullers to make the plate over six days.

PAIR OF TONGS

You cannot have enough pairs of tongs. It is most important that the left hand is comfortable holding work in tongs, so that you can concentrate on what is going on at the other end of the bar. If the left hand is struggling to hold the tongs, ill-fitting unsuitably on something they were not designed to hold, the right hand cannot hit the metal effectively.

Some manufacturers sell tongs that are too big and heavy for everyday use, so it is a good idea to be able to make your own. For most creative smithing, small tongs are quite adequate. Heavy tongs just add to the strain of holding the work, which is hard enough without added burden.

If you can make one pair of tongs, you can make any type. Mild steel is adequate for some tongs, but it is better to use something rather harder, such as reinforcing bar, which is half-hard. Small pieces of scrap 'rebar' (reinforcing bar) can be found, sometimes, at construction sites or in scrap yards.

OPPOSITE: **Hammering the jaw of the flat bit tong over the edge of the anvil. The hammer must hit over the edge of the anvil, half on, squashing the jaw and half off, pushing the eye down.**

Flat bit tongs

As a practice piece, try making a pair of tongs from mild steel. 400×16 square will make a pair of tongs. This type of tongs described is 'flat bit' – the most common tongs. It is useful to thin out the end of the jaw, so that it can be used to prise open hot metal or to lever things.

Jaws

Heat the end of the bar until orange, and place about 25 over the edge of the anvil, at a part where there is a sharp edge. With the hammer half over the edge, flatten the jaw of the tong until it is half the thickness – 8 thick. The hammer is squashing the jaw, but pushing the rest down over the edge. The jaw will expand out to about 25 wide. It will also lengthen. Now thin out the end of the jaw to about 3 thick, for prising open hot metal or for levering.

Next, heat the bar again, and place the blade at 45 degrees on the opposite side of the anvil, and turn the bar a quarter turn to the left. Look at the edge of the anvil, and adjust the bar until it makes an arrow shape with the edge of the anvil. The jaw is now vertical. Hit the bar, with the hammer half over the edge, until the eye of the tongs is half of the thickness of the bar. It will also expand to about 25 wide. Continue the blows back from the eye for about another inch. At this point, the jaw will have turned up several degrees.

Place the eye in the vice, and knock the jaw down until it is at right angles to the eye. It will also have bent out of line, so straighten it, too.

Tongs: distortion from forging placed in vice jaws to be rectified. The eye is gripped and the jaw is hammered down level with the top of the vice.

Tongs: forming eye over edge of anvil. The angle just formed makes an arrow head with the edge of the anvil.

Heat the bar again, and place again over the far side of the anvil, again turning through 90 degrees to the left. Push the eye over the edge, until it is slightly further over than the width of the eye. Do not make it too long. It has to end up round, after punching the hole. If it is too long, the geometry of the eye will not work. Knock the bar down again, until the bar is half the width of the eye – 12. Check the rest of the forging for squareness and thicknesses. If the eye is tapered in thickness – as it probably will be – make sure that it is uniform.

Tongs: making eye. Note overhang is very slightly longer than width of metal. Note, too, the slight taper at the end of the jaw, used for levering things apart.

The eye will be square cornered. Heat it, and place over the edge of the anvil upright. Moving the bar back over the anvil, hit the corner, rounding the corners. Now you must repeat the process, making another tong on the other end of the bar. Do try to make them symmetrical. You will improve with practice.

the bar. Swages are better, but you might not have them.

The rounding off should end about 50 from the eye. The rectangular part next to the eye should be blended into the round rein. This part of the rein is subjected to most of the strain, so it is left larger.

Tongs: rounding off the rein stops two inches from eye. The metal thickens slightly up to the eye, giving more strength where there is most leverage.

When this blending is complete, place the eye over the far edge of the anvil, and knock the eye down. This will make the reins have a gap at the top, which will allow the tongs to hang over a rod with the reins vertical. Commercially-manufactured tongs tend to hang with the reins sticking out dangerously.

Tongs: rounding eye after forging. The left hand swings the rein back and forth while the hammer rounds the eye.

Reins

Having made the jaws of the tongs, now it is time to draw out the reins. There is a lot of work to do here, and if you can enlist a striker, the job is halved.

Place the work over the beak of the anvil, and draw down the bar until it is about 11 square. Finish it, rounding off on the face of the anvil. You can use flatters, but they will tend to flatten

Tongs: bending the eye down from the rein. This gives a gap at the hanging point when the tongs are assembled.

PUNCHING THE HOLE

This process is always done when everything else has been done. If you punch the hole, and then modify the jaws, or straighten the reins, or anything else, the eye-hole will distort. Putting it right will enlarge it, making the rivet slack.

To punch the hole, use your round punch, and proceed as with the hole in the hanging basket bracket back plate (*see* Chapter 7). Hang the jaw over the edge of the anvil, and punch in the centre. When nearly through, turn it, and punch through the punch hole. When you turn it over, the first side of the punched hole will probably be distorted. There is a little tool – and it works a treat by supporting the eye when remaking the hole. Make sure that your preferred rivet fits easily though the hole.

Tongs: punching eyehole. This must be the last job after every other stage; if anything else is done afterwards, the eye can be distorted, and rounding it off will enlarge it, making the rivet slack.

Finishing hole over punch hole.

Special tool for rounding off punched holes. As the punch enters the eye from the second side, the first hole will distort; punching gently through from each side over this tool will support the eye and round the hole.

RIVETING

It is easy to lose rivets, when heating them in the fire. In the furnace, they are more traceable. However, the following method keeps them where they should be: put the rivet in one of the tongs, and put that in the fire. It cannot escape, unless you turn the tong over.

When you bring the tong, with the rivet, out of the fire, put it upside down, carefully, on the face of the anvil, so the leg of the rivet is sticking up. Place the other tong on to the rivet, and gently hit the edge of the rivet, round and round, with the ball peen of an engineer's hammer. If you hit the rivet square on, it will expand in the hole, and rivet the tongs together permanently. By hitting the edge, it creates another head. Quickly open and close the reins to maintain looseness.

Checking rivet for size.

Adjustments

Irregularities in manufacture will now show themselves. The reins will probably cross over, and the jaws will have to be aligned. Heat up the whole jaw area, and make sure that all is aligned. If the jaws do not close, warm them up, place a round punch between the reins, and hit the jaws until they do close.

Apart from tapering the front of the jaw, another tip is to heat the jaws, place a piece of 6 wire between the jaws, and hit them. This will create grooves in the jaws, which will enable

Tongs: finishing the ends of the reins. After rounding off, a gentle flat is made at the last 40, making sure there are no burrs.

Tongs: finishing ends of reins with a gentle tap over the end of the anvil. This will help to stop the hands slipping off, and will also take a link to keep the reins together, rather than straining with the left hand.

you to grip small round pieces. Not only that, but it will stop the face of the jaw becoming convex, and losing grip.

If the ends of the reins are heated, and flattened slightly, widening the ends, they look better, and making sure that the very ends are rounded off to prevent chafing completes a good-looking pair of tongs. Tipping the ends out a little stops the hand slipping off, and allows a link to be used for keeping the tongs gripping tightly, taking the strain off the left hand. If you are struggling with gripping, you are not concentrating on what you are hitting.

UPSETTING

Drawing the reins down from the original material size is hard work. Another way is to make the jaws from the stock as before, and weld on some smaller, round bar. This was always done in the past, when time was short. Enough material must be left on the jaw to make a scarf.

The end of the rein is then upset to make a scarf also. To upset the end of the rein, place the heated end horizontally in the vice with about 20 sticking out. Quickly hit the end, compressing it, and thickening. Upsetting is more difficult when the material is thinner as it will invariably bend. Take it out of the vice, heat, and straighten up on the anvil. During straightening, you will make the bar square. This is good, for that is how it should be. It will probably need two or three goes at upsetting before the end is large enough to make a scarf. Also, make sure that the bar adjacent to the scarf is upset, because during welding, some of the metal will waste away due to overheating.

Place the heated end of the upset over the near side of the anvil, and hit down, compressing the end and pushing the rest down, leaving a thicker part. Now hit the end with the hammer at an angle to thin out the end, and tap the back of the scarf down.

Welded tongs: piece of 20 square forged into a jaw, leaving enough metal to form a scarf.

Try to make the two scarves identical. Place them together, hot, and make sure that they fit. Now heat them in a clean fire, with the scarves down. Watch for the white bursting sparks, and when they are hot, bring them out, place together, and weld. It is important that the scarves are placed on the anvil so that the hammer brings them together – not pushing them apart. Heat the joined scarves again, and forge in the ends of the scarves, one at a time. Forge the joint, making it disappear.

(For more on upsetting, *see* Chapter 7.)

ABOVE RIGHT: **Forming scarf over anvil's edge.**

ABOVE: **Tongs: ready for welding after making scarves. The piece to be welded must be placed on the anvil so that the hammer hits the weld and pushes it together; in this case, the jaw would go beneath the rein so the hammer pushes the rein towards the smith.**

RIGHT: **Welding the tongs: Several heats may be necessary to completely blend the jaw to the rein.**

Other types of tongs

As mentioned previously, it is useful to have different sizes and shapes of tongs, so the left hand is comfortably guiding the end to be forged, not struggling to hold an ill-fitting pair of tongs.

Box tongs

Box tongs are needed in many sizes, so here is how to make them.

Forge the ends of the jaws as before, but make one of them twice as long. Cut down the centre of this jaw with a hot sett. Place the jaw in the vice with the split end out. Prise the parts apart with the blade of the hot sett. Now place the jaw in the vice with the open part sticking up, and bend it at right angles, to form the 'cheek'. Heat the jaw again, and place a piece of the stock bar in the vice with the jaw, resting on the bent cheek. Bend the other cheek down onto the stock bar. Leave enough of the cheek to grip the bar, and trim off any surplus. Make up the tongs as before.

Box tongs: bending first cheek in vice.

Box tongs: cutting jaw with hot sett.

Box tongs: bending second cheek over a length of the bar which they are to hold.

Hollow bits

Hollow bits are made the same way as flat bits, but, depending upon what size of material is to be held, the jaws may need to be wider. After making the jaws, they need to be bent into a right angle. You can use a piece of angle steel bar as the former, and a piece of square bar as the upper former. The jaws are set on the desired section of bar after assembly.

Bolt tongs

These are used for holding pieces, such as bolts, which have an enlarged end (head). They are an alternative to hollow bits for holding round or square bars.

The jaws must be about three times the length of flat bit jaws. The part of the jaw leading from the eye is flat, but quite thick, and the actual gripping part of the jaw is thinner, and wider. It needs to be bent in the same way as the hollow bits. With time, and collection of tools, a square bottom swage and a cold sett can be used for this operation.

Scroll tongs, or round pliers

These tongs are for putting great pressure on scrolls in confined spaces, so it is necessary to use stronger material. The aforementioned rebar is ideal.

Forge the rebar into 20 × 10. As it is going to be forged all over, it is not necessary to dress the surface. Forge the end down to a bullet shape. Leave a section for the eye, 22 long, and make the rein. Be sure to leave the part next to the eye larger, then draw the rein out square, rounding off later. Push the eye down as before, to make the tongs hang over a rod. Dress all surfaces, and finally punch the holes. Rivet up. Make the ends symmetrical, and bring them into line, then tip the ends of the reins out a little.

Scroll tongs, showing the shape of the jaws, which are made from reinforcing bar to ensure they are harder.

Bow pliers

Again make these out of rebar. The method is the same as for scroll tongs, but the jaws are slightly longer. Both of these specialist tongs are very useful.

Bow pliers: The two tongs are made straight and matched exactly, then bent into shape, and then the hole is punched.

Links

Occasionally, it is useful to have a link holding the reins together, so that all responsibility is taken off the left hand. It is therefore advisable to know how to make links. It is a good idea to have several of these links, of varying lengths.

Find a short piece of wire, 6 diameter. You will need about 125. Heat it all, using the groove in the flat bit tongs to hold it.

Bend the hot wire into a U shape, with equal legs. Bend the ends around the beak until they

Making link. Having several links of different lengths is useful for gripping tongs, so start at about 85, and take successive lengths 10 longer each time.

overlap. Prise them apart. Heat one end, and make a depression over the corner of the anvil. Repeat on the other end, making sure that the two depressions coincide. Bring the two ends, now closed, to welding heat, and weld over the face of the anvil. To round off the weld, and make it look good, use the end of the beak.

ABOVE: **With the link opened out a little, place the end over the corner of the anvil face and tap gently to form a depression, then repeat with the other end.**

LEFT: **Weld the two parts together on the face of the anvil, and finish rounding off over the beak.**

LEAVES AND ORGANIC FORMS

Though this chapter is about leaves and organic forms, it will also expand your repertoire of tools and techniques. Since the mid-1970s in Britain there have been practitioners in ironwork who have freed themselves from traditional work, and there has been a revolution in production of interesting products. Some of the following techniques might help to achieve your ideas.

Making a leaf

Take a piece of 20 × 6 flat, and point the end. This can be done either by cutting off a triangular piece, or by forging it to a point. Next, forge the end down, so that it is pointed in both planes. Make sure that the end is offset to one side.

Next put the bar on the beak, about 35 over the edge. Now hit the bar, in a vertical position, on the beak, forging it square. Taper the bar behind the square, back about 75. Take the corners off the square, rounding it off slightly, and blend these into the flat bar. Putting the end of the leaf right next to the end of the beak, just tip the end of the leaf in the opposite direction.

Taking a round faced hammer, hit the sides of the leaf, spreading them out sideways, while

OPPOSITE: **Simple leaf: cutting taper off with hot sett.**

Leaf, showing offset; this leaf has been tapered in both planes, and the end is half the original thickness. It was placed with the straight side down, and hammered with the top side remaining almost straight.

leaving a ridge along the middle of the leaf. It should be possible to make this ridge curved, by careful hammering. Ensure that the edges of the leaf are smooth, with no bumps, and with more care, eliminate any surface imperfections. This will improve with practice.

Blending the taper into the flat bar, making the taper longer.

Bending the very end of the tip the other way.

Putting some life into a leaf.

Creating the ridge down the middle of the leaf, using a round-faced hammer. Have the work near the edge of the anvil to get the edge really thin when finishing off.

Large leaf, showing veins created by a curved fuller.

You now have a leaf, but to make it more lively, give it some three dimensional movement by tipping the end over the beak and waving the sides with the peen of the hammer. Where the stem of the leaf is rounded, it can also be twisted through 90 degrees. This means that several leaves can be welded together to form twigs.

Sometimes, larger leaves are required, and, because they are large, further marks representing veins can be made on the surface. Using a piece of 40 × 8 cut the end off at 45 degrees (it is too much to draw down) and make the leaf as before, but stop short of shaping with the round faced hammer. An interesting way is to shape one side, creating the ridge down the centre of the leaf, and then make veins on the other half. Using a 10 or 12 fuller, make grooves from the ridge outwards, preferably curving slightly as you go. Then the leaf can be given some life again.

Iris leaf with edges hammered thin. Use the edge of the anvil to achieve the fine edge.

triangular piece 75 × 25 off one end. Shape the edges into a regular, symmetrical form. Because the leaf is supposed to be very thin, hammer all of the edges with a round faced hammer, until they are 1.5 thick.

Iris leaf with taper cut.

Iris leaf

This leaf illustrates a technique that can be used in many applications apart from leaves. To make the iris leaf, take a piece of 30×6×375 and cut a

Grooving tool, with cold sett.

A GROOVING TOOL AND
A COLD SETT

Next, you will need to make another tool, a grooving tool, which will come in useful for other jobs. It consists of two short pieces of 20 round bar, about 50 long. Their ends will need to be rounded off so that they will not mark any work being done. They should be (electric) welded onto a piece of 30 square bar (or whatever size fits your hardie hole).

At this point, you will also need a cold sett. If you have not got one, this is a good excuse to make one, as they prove useful, too. It is the same process a making the fuller, but the end is finished at 90 degrees instead of rounding off.

Grooving tool making groove in iris leaf.

Heat the leaf, and carefully place it aligned with the groove between the two round bars. You might have to prop the leaf, or enlist some assistance. However, make a groove right down the leaf, in the centre. The leafing hammer can also be used to start the grooving process. Observation will tell you that the iris leaf is not flat from the centre vein to the outside. We use the two curved surfaces of the new grooving tool to curve our leaf outwards. Make sure that the sides are smooth and uniform. Now the end of the leaf and, to a lesser extent, the body of the leaf can be curved over the beak. Because of the thickness of the centre, the leaf will make a graceful curve, and not crease

Alternative method of starting groove, using leafing stake and leafing hammer.

Iris leaf, showing graceful curve which can be achieved with thickened centre and thinned edges. The edges have been curved back over the grooving tool.

across like a blade of grass. The thickening cannot be seen – only the thinned edges. This method of creating gentle curves in (apparently) very thin steel can be used in many other applications.

Water leaf

These leaves, much in vogue in the eighteenth century, are rarely used today, but they are fun to make. To really get the feeling for water leaves, historical ironwork should be studied. There are traditional situations where leaves were added, sometimes in pairs.

There are several ways to make them, but you should bear in mind the previous example of the iris leaf. Although they look very thin, they will be more easily made, and curved into shape, if they are thicker in the centre. Two methods are described here. With the first, the method most commonly taught, the leaf base wraps around the scroll, or whatever it is attached to, and is fire-welded into place. With the second method, described briefly later, the leaf is made from a solid bar.

Water leaves need to be made from something softer than the usual sheet metal workers' mild steel, which is very hard and keeps

Advanced leafing stake, showing water leaf pushed through to enable leafing hammer to be used downwards.

its shape when bent at right angle for engineering purposes. Deep drawing steel is just the thing, if you can get it. It is used in engineering applications which require the metal to flex and stretch during manufacture, such as making body panels for the motor industry. That is quite soft. Another material, which is even softer, is pure iron. These materials, however, are not always readily available.

A drawing should be made first on paper. This is then transferred to the metal surface. It is best if the surface is slightly rusty. You need a piece of brown paper, which will have to be coated with soft blackboard chalk. Place the brown paper, chalk downward, on the metal, and the drawing on top. They should all be kept firmly in position by sticky tape. Carefully go over the drawing with a pencil, making sure that you have covered every part. Remove the drawing and brown paper, and you should have the drawing in chalk, which then needs emphasizing with engineer's chalk.

The outline should then be followed with a cold chisel, and the leaf cut out. Of course, there are quicker ways of doing this, such as plasma cutting and laser cutting, but we are assuming here that expensive equipment is not at hand.

The edges should be filed to remove sharp parts, and then the leaf is ready for heating. Thinning the edges will expand the size of the leaf a little, and this will need to be taken into consideration when making the drawing. It is usually advised to use 3 thick material but 5 can be better. It is up to you to try it out. The edges should be taken down to 1.5 thick, but no thinner at this point. Further thinning will take place later in the finishing of the process. The round-faced hammer will be used for this thinning. Ensure that the edges are smooth shaped, with no bumps.

The socket

The first heating should make the socket, which is ultimately welded onto the scroll. To find the exact size of the socket, the scroll material should be applied to the surface of the leaf material, and turned through 360 degrees, which gives the length of the surface. Then

MAKING A LEAFING STAKE

Now you will need a leafing stake. Most of these tools are quite simple, and can be made with tools you have already made. The easy leafing stake is just a piece of 25 square, split down with a hot sett, and hammered, then filed, into shape.

If you are contemplating further exercises in leaf work, there is an improved version of the leaf stake, which takes more time to make, but allows extra curling on special leaves.

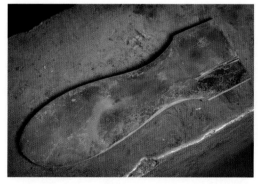

Line marked on leaf socket, showing position of leaf for making socket.

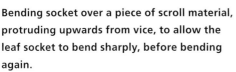

Bending socket over a piece of scroll material, protruding upwards from vice, to allow the leaf socket to bend sharply, before bending again.

Creating the first groove in the leaf section with a leafing hammer.

add twice the thickness of the material. That length is the total width of the socket. Mark half of the major side next to the centre line of the leaf.

Heat the socket material, and have to hand a short length of the scroll material, such as a 25 × 12. Bring the hot socket out of the fire, and place in the vice with the scroll section next to the top of the vice jaw, on the marked line. Hit the outstanding section of the scroll down, over the bar which will need to be held above the jaw, to allow the socket to bend again. Heat the socket again, and bring the other side of

the socket down over the bar. Next, heat again, and bring the smaller sides down onto the bar. They should almost meet in the middle. Heat again, and form crisp corners on the socket.

The socket can now be used as a handle, with flat bit tongs. Be very careful not to overheat the leaf, especially the edges. The fire should be turned down for this job. With a complete heat, place the leaf on the stake, and, with a leafing hammer, knock the centre down into the stake, creating a channel. The material will probably want to go asymmetrical, but moving the leaf from side to side, presenting 'long' sides to the valley, and hitting the leaf

Straightening edge of leaf, which always distorts.

down into the channel, you can level the leaf. During this process, the leaf edges will distort, so they will need to be straightened on the anvil face.

Fine-tuning the leaves

Curling

Having made the whole of the leaf into a groove, it is now time to curl it up. Direct the hammer to the side of the leafing stake, pushing the leaf material over the edge into a curve. Making this shape causes the outer edges to stretch, so it is hard work. Also, because it is so thin it will cool very quickly. You will need many heats. There is also a tendency to go off to one side, and corrections will have to be made.

It is necessary to curl the leaf more than shown in the drawing, because when the crimps are put in, the leaf body will tend to straighten. Occasionally, you may need to use the beak of

Curling the leaf over the edge of the leafing stake.

MAKING A CRIMPING STAKE

This stake is necessary for creating the wavy edges of the water leaves, which are inspired by *Potamogeton Crispus*, found in aquaria and fresh water ponds. As the edges are of constant pitch, it is worth spending some time on the convex curves as well as the concave ones. The stakes can be made any size, but there is a tendency to make them too small.

Take a piece of large material, 40×20 or so. Forge one end so that it fits either in the hardie hole or in the vice. Using a piece of 20 diameter bar, make a depression in the centre of the bar, about halfway down. Then round off the sides with a hammer, taking the roundness right round to vertical. Finally finish with a file.

Crimping stake.

the anvil for further bending, or straightening, if the leaf goes astray. Inadvertent curves in the sides of the leaf may be straightened on the face of the anvil before going on to make crimps.

Crimping

Looking at natural leaves, the veins almost always reach forward from the centre vein. This piece of observation seems to pass by the majority of people. However, it should be borne in mind when crimping our leaves.

Try the exercise cold, before heating. The leaf should be offered to the crimping stake at an angle, to make the forward reaching veins. Bring the hammer down accurately into the groove. An aide to this technique is to thrust the elbow firmly against the ribcage, to stop lateral movement.

Beside the depression, the sides will form a radius from the crimping tool. This depression must now be placed at the outer radius of the crimping stake, bringing the next vein into position. Careful positioning thus ensures that the pitch of the crimps is constant. Make sure that the angle is maintained. Because of the thin material, it will cool, probably before the second vein can be made.

After completing one side, start the other. It is easy to get the veins out of synch, so be very careful to make the depressions symmetrical. It will probably take a few attempts to get the symmetry.

Check the shape of the leaf against the drawing. Adjust any discrepancies. Now take the scroll, to which the leaf will be welded. Check that the socket fits perfectly, but easily. It is no help to find that the leaf will not fit when it is hot.

Crimping stake in use, making wavy edges to water leaf with a leafing hammer.

Welding leaf to scroll

The procedure is to heat the thick-bodied scroll almost to welding temperature, then add the thin-bodied leaf for complete heating. This ensures that the whole thing achieves welding temperature together. Otherwise, the leaf might burn off while the scroll is heating. Another point to bear in mind here is that the thicker the socket material, the more heat it will stand while achieving welding temperature.

Have a wire brush handy to clean the scroll properly. Heat the scroll, keeping the leaf near the fire to pre-warm. Watch for the white, bursting sparks coming from the scroll, withdraw, wire brush, and slip the leaf over the scroll. Now quickly put it back in the fire, and see the sparks again. Make sure that the parts to be welded are not too far into the fire, so as to preserve the leaf and its delicate crimps.

Put the fizzing leaf on the anvil, and quickly weld the leaf on to the scroll, turning every two or three blows. If it has not welded, the scroll and leaf will begin to appear as different colours. If it has welded, it will feel solid, so hammer the socket, blending the leaf into the socket. It will probably have to be welded to another piece of bar, so do not overdo the blending. You must leave enough metal for the scarf.

WATER LEAF FROM A SOLID BAR (ALTERNATIVE METHOD)

Another way to make water leaves is to start with a solid bar, say, 25 × 12. This must be hammered out sideways, using a cross-peen hammer for speed, until it is at least 50, preferably 60 wide. The centre of the leaf can be left quite thick..

Instead of a socket, the solid is left, and this saves time, and ensures that there is plenty of metal to be welded. The leaf is marked out and cut as before, and the forming follows the same procedure. After welding, the beginning of the crimped edge is gently eased around the sides of the scroll bar, and the leaf base is blended in.

Composite flower

Many tasks in crafts require patience. Sometimes there is a need for several pieces, which should match. Making them exactly the same is rarely required, but it is a skill which can pay dividends. Flower petals look better when they match. This exercise requires six petals, and six little spikes, all of which will be welded onto a stem.

Take a piece of 13 × 3 flat bar, in a handling length of about 600. Forge one end to a point, and about 100 from that point, forge the material into a square shape. Hammer the edges flatter, to about half the thickness.

For a first attempt, make the petals simple. Later, more complicated designs can be applied to the petals, but, when making a first delicate weld, things can go wrong.

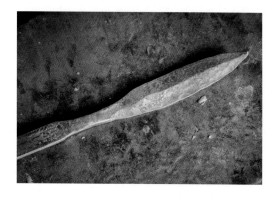

Small leaf with stem forged to be welded onto tapered bar.

The little spikes should be made from 6 round wire. They need to be 150 long. Make a taper at one end, about 25 long. (This is where the groove in the flat bit tong jaws comes in useful.)

The stem of the flower is made from 10 round wire. A long taper should be made on the stem, making the end 6 diameter – the same as the spikes. Now bend the tapered end of the spikes slightly, so that the spikes lie flat on the stem but follow the taper and lie around the end of the taper, touching. Some means of temporary attachment is needed now. Traditionally, it would be soft iron wire, but that is not readily available. Provided it can be kept away from the flames, either a plastic tie-wrap, or a length of strong tape can be used to hold the spikes together.

A tight, small fire is needed here. It is best to have small coke, only bean-sized, with a welding zone very small too, like a walnut if possible. Make sure that the fire is clean. Get the fire up to welding temperature, and place the ends just into the welding zone, to preserve the tape. Remember that the stem, inside, will take longer to heat. If necessary, have a can of water to hand, to keep the tape cool while the weld heats.

When welding seven parts together, it is important to place the hot bar on the anvil with three components vertically in line so that all three are welded with one blow. Quickly turn through 60 degrees and weld the next, and the third. When this weld has taken, and the metal is still hot, hit quickly while turning the metal, and forge the round section in. (The

Spikes ready for welding vertically in line, to weld through all three.

tape will have melted off now, having done its job.) Reheat the weld, up to welding temperature again, and now it will feel solid. Continue to forge the taper down, so that the petals can be laid on as the spikes were. Be careful not to overdo it!

With the weld cool, offer the petals up to the taper, to check that they fit. Adjust if necessary. Again, use something to attach the petals, as before. Repeat the welding process.

SMALL COKE CLINKER

A word of warning: when using small coke for fine welds, it seems to clinker up rather more, so check the fire for clinker before attempting the second weld.

Having welded the petals, it is time to arrange them into a flower. This is quite tricky, and requires a very clean fire, or possibly the use of Oxy-propane, or Oxy-acetylene flames, in order to avoid clinkering up. The scroll tongs will be used for this process.

For a super-flower, if you can find a squat-ball swage, you can weld a piece of 6×13 around the end of the welded petals. This is difficult. The flat section is cut to length, and wrapped around the weld. It is essential that the heat is concentrated at the end, by having a small fire, or the petals will burn off. If the wrapped piece is applied after the centre is heated, it will not take so long to heat.

For the next stage you really need an assistant to do this job, because it needs three hands. Have the squat-ball swage ready, with a

Squat ball swage, for making ball over the weld.

hammer, on the top of the anvil. Bring out the piece to be welded, wire-brush, and put straight into the swage, while your mate hits rapidly. Turn the metal constantly, as it welds, then forms the ball. The excess metal will be extruded from the ball swage. Trim this to about 20, and carefully saw it twice, to form four little spikes. These can be heated gently, and bent backwards. This forms a flower seed pod. Then the petals and spikes can be bent back as before.

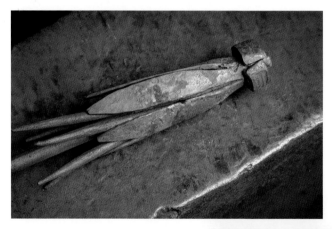

ABOVE: **Length of flat bar wrapped around weld, to make squat ball.**

RIGHT: **Excess metal extruded from end of seed pod by ball swage.**

HANGING BASKET BRACKET

When we discussed basic techniques in Chapter 2, the method of marking out and splitting was explained using a back plate as an example. Here we finish the back plate, and make the rest of the bracket. This exercise uses several different techniques, in addition to the ones explained already.

The hook

As this hook will be riveted to a scroll, it is made from square material. We start with 600×12 square. Having made a taper on the previous job (leaves and petals), we will use the same method. However, the procedure is slightly different.

A round cross-section is used for the actual hook, which ends with a transition to square. The hook's parts are roughly 75 for the taper, 50 for the round, cylindrical part, and 25 for the transition from round to square. To make things simpler, take a centre-punch and while it is still cold mark, from the end of the bar, 75, 50 and 25 lengths.

Make a short taper, keeping the material square. By making a short taper, the material is forced out in a convex curve at the end. If

OPPOSITE: **Elongated bullet shape of taper for snail scroll on the end of the hook. Also shown is the bar marked out: 75, 50 and 25 – the parts of the hook before forging.**

the tapering is done gradually, the sides of the bar will overhang, forming a hole in the middle, called 'piping', which can cause problems when drawing down to a fine point, as it shreds like a green twig.

The taper starts again with the 75 over the beak, and is drawn down, leaving the end about 3 across as before. Whereas the last taper was a long cone, this one will need to be like an elongated bullet (shown with the bar marked 75, 50 and 25).

Next the 50 portion needs to be rounded off, into a cylinder. Try to avoid placing the metal beyond the punch mark. This can be helped by placing the back end of the metal against the thigh. The surface of the last inch will be untouched.

Leave the final taper until the end. Fine points are likely to burn.

The last 25 is for the transition from square to round. Put the last dot next to the edge of the anvil, and, sloping the face of the hammer, create a long triangle on the upper corner. The anvil will make a similar, smaller triangle underneath. Repeat on all corners. Blend the triangles in gently with the hammer, revolving the metal slightly for each blow.

As the taper is to be forged into a snail shape, the material must go quite quickly from very fine at the end to large. The shape we are about to create is a naturally-occurring phenomenon; apart from molluscs, it is in hurricanes, flower seeds and many other instances in nature. It has been used in ironwork for a very long time.

Now we use the little radius on the anvil for another purpose. Place the heated metal 6 over the radius and gently bend it over the edge; it is important not to squash the round cross-section. Next, put the hammer at 45 degrees to the metal and tap it gently, while pushing the bar over the edge. This will make a parabola, because the resistance to bending increases as the section increases.

When reheating this parabola, it is essential to place it in the fire with the thin end up. Let the tip emerge, just out of the coke. Waggle it, so that you can see it. When this end is hot, the rest will be.

Creating parabolic bend over the edge of the anvil, where it is curved at the left end.

Long thin triangle made in transition from square to round section.

Making the 'snail' for the hook

The snail is an involute curve. The technique for bending it needs some practice while the metal is cold. Place the metal horizontally on the anvil, with the parabola upward. Take the hammer, and hold it horizontally, addressing the curve. While slowly raising the metal with the left hand, gently tap the curved end, bringing the hammer over the top of the curve

Finished parabola, placed upon the anvil after heating, with the left hand level with the anvil and the hammer held horizontally. The left hand is raised, while the hammer hits very gently, and gradually rises to vertical.

Amount of point to hang over radius on anvil to start curling the snail scroll.

Creating snail: bringing left hand up, while hammering over the top.

anti-clockwise until it is vertical. This will curve the end in. Repeat, and as the end curves in, bringing thicker sections into play, hit the curve harder for the first two or three blows. The metal should be touching the inside of the curve as it curls up. Be careful not to get carried away; keep the end in proportion.

Bending the hook

To make the hook shape, we employ another frequently-used tool: the fork. Such a simple thing, but indispensable. Heat the metal, and put the curled end next to the fork. Bend the metal towards you, then move it away about 12, and bend again. Repeat twice.

If the metal were pulled right round, it would assume the radius of the fork prong. This is too narrow. By pushing

the metal forward, a greater radius is made. By bringing the snail back to the fork, and bending back, this radius can be reduced.

Using fork to curve hook.

Now take another heat, further along the hook. Quench the part that is finished, and place this (cold and therefore hard) part in the fork. Pull the end around, until the hot metal is closer than the width of the bulbous part of the hook.

Lift it off the fork, replace it the other way and pull it back to finish the hook.

Hook lifted off fork, and bent back.

Making a back plate

The back plate described in this book is a traditional shape, and has been used for centuries, for example, where a load has to be spread, such as in weak walls of buildings, to prevent bulging, or where something heavy has to be supported. The beginning of the process of making a back plate was described at the end of Chapter 2.

USING THE HOT SETT

The hot sett is a finer chisel than the cold chisel, because it is going to cut through hot metal.

Sharpening

Many manufacturers do not seem to sharpen the edges of the blade, but it is useful to do it (see Chapter 4). When cutting, this leaves a V end to the cut. This is not only aesthetically more pleasant, but it is stronger, too.

Making your own

 Most people buy hot setts, but these are generally made like an axe, with the blade parallel to the handle. If you make your own, forge the blade 30 degrees to the shaft. Apart from moving the holding hand away from any heat in the bar, it enables the user to see the back edge of the sett, and to ensure that it is following the line. Of course, left-handed users will need the opposite angle. However, if the smith is cutting with the assistance of a striker, using a sledge-hammer, he will need a left-handed sett in his right hand.

Cooling

Hot setts should be cooled every three or four blows, or they might soften.

Heavy vs light hammering

Often in hammering it is better to start using a light hammer so as not to tire the arm. Tiredness comes with loss of blood sugar during repeated hammering, but when using the hot sett, the hammer must be struck only after checking that the sett is in the right place, so the blows are at half the pace and the blood sugar depletion will not be as much. Therefore, a heavier hammer can be used for these intermittent blows, and a heavier hammer will hasten the sett through the bar.

Saving the blade

Remember that care must be taken when the sett is nearly through. It is very easy to cut right through the bar and strike the anvil with the blade, flattening the edge. Even though the blade is hard, the anvil is hard too, and because it is bigger, it wins.

A piece of flat plate, about 3 thick, should be employed under the bar to prevent the blade hitting the anvil. When the sett is nearly through, cut from the end nearest you. The two parts will spread apart until you reach the end. Make sure the split goes right through, so the cut is clean. The cutting plate will soon be covered with splits and marks, so discard it before it makes lots of nasty marks on the underside of the bar.

Creating the flat scrolls

Having cut the split, it is time to curve the scrolls. Only cut one end, because the box tongs will not accommodate the split end – it widens.

To open up the two parts of the scrolls, they will need hitting on the inside of the split, but the other half is in the way, so place the heated bar on the far edge of the anvil and knock the left hand side down.

First quadrant of the scroll, made where the beak is 50 diameter. All of the hammer blows are on the end of the bar, using the added leverage, and no hammer marks are on the quadrant.

One side of the cut knocked down over the anvil, out of the way of the hammer used to make the flat scroll.

Now the other side can be curled. Place the bar, vertically, on the beak, at the point where the beak's diameter is about 50. Hit the far end, to use the leverage, and finish when the end is at right angles. During the bending, the flat will twist, because it does not like bending on edge. It will need flattening each time it is hit. There should be no hammer marks on the edge of this first quadrant. It has no taper. Only hit the end of the split piece.

Be especially careful to keep the bar at that 50 part of the beak, otherwise the radius will diminish. The work tends to creep down the taper.

Take another heat and, hitting the end again, knock the bar further round the beak. When

Hanging the curve under the beak, after the curve is beyond a right angle. The taper is made more easily when the hammer is hit downwards.

CREATING A CURVE

Now hit the bar from the quadrant to the end, squashing the metal to taper it. It is most important, at this point, to realize that, in creating a curve, no two blows should land on the same place. That would make a flat.

The metal should be kept moving by the left hand, while the hammer hits above the anvil at the same place. As you hammer the curve, note the flat surface at the end of the bar. It will 'gather', which means that the metal thickens at the edges, forming a groove down the middle. You must flatten this before it joins to form a sharp line, which will blemish the surface.

Keep tapering until a fine point is made. This often results in a straight line, pointing somewhere. However, if you use the technique used to create the snail on the hook, bringing the hammer around the end of the curve, while bringing the curve round, you will get the curve to finish beautifully into itself.

Creating the curved taper. The left hand must be kept moving constantly to create a curved surface.

Bringing the curve right round, into itself.

Repeat the process for the other side, and when it is finished, the box tongs will fit over the curves, and allow the whole thing to start again.

Both sides finished, enabling the box tongs to fit again.

it has gone further than a right angle, hang it from the underside, so that you are hitting downwards.

If the metal does slip down the beak, a narrow bend will occur. It is very puzzling to see how to rectify this; however, using lateral thinking, we hang the hot bend over the beak and hit the body of the back plate on its edge, opening the bend so that it can be finished.

Bearing in mind the fact that the anvil makes marks on the underside of the metal. It is important to remember to keep the bar vertical over the beak, so that the other side of the edge will be at right angles to the flat surface. Also, when scrolling the ends, the bar should be at right angles to an imaginary tangent to the beak, for the same reason.

Marking the points where the scrolls touch the edge of the anvil, which is where the holes will be made for the fixing screws.

Square-headed screws look good when attaching the bracket to the wall, and mean that the holes in the plate are not countersunk.

PREVENTING CASE HARDENING

During the making of these curved ends, the metal will be going in and out of the fire a number of times. As mentioned earlier, iron likes to combine with other elements. When it is in a coke fire, it is absorbing carbon into the surface. If the metal is quenched, having absorbed carbon, it will harden sufficiently (case hardening) to blunt the drill, which is needed to make the fastening holes. Therefore, do not quench any of the curls; let them cool naturally, which stops them from hardening.

When the metal has cooled, check that the curved ends are symmetrical, and offer the curves to a flat edge (usually the anvil). Mark the points where they touch, and draw a chalk line. Divide this line, and centre punch for the fastening holes, which are used to attach the bracket to the wall. After drilling, use a larger drill to remove burrs on both sides of the plate.

Punching the square hole

To make a neat connection between the hook and the back plate, we punch a square hole. Historically railings and gates were always punched, with balusters (uprights) passing through rails (horizontals). This contrasts

Swelling on back plate, which enables the size of the hole to be reduced while still hot.

with the modern, cheap, untidy way of doing connections – welding around the baluster.

Punching is done hot, and the punch is quite long, about 250–300. This length is only for keeping the hand away from the hot metal. The end of the punch is traditionally flat, and it needs to be about 6 across. If it is any broader, it will not easily go through the metal, and if it is narrower, it could overheat, making it soft. This could cause it to 'mushroom' inside the hole being punched, there to remain for ever.

On our job, the punched hole should be about 25 away from the split at one end of the back plate. Mark the distance with chalk, then make a centre-punch mark about 3 across. This will show when it is hot.

Grip the plate with the box tongs, and heat it. Place the plate horizontally in the fire, so that it takes an even heat. When hot, place upon the anvil, brush the surface to remove dust and clinker, and carefully place the end of the punch on the hole.

Hit the punch with a heavy hammer. Check to see if the new mark is square. If it is, punch again. If it is not, re-set the punch square, and hit again.

Keep punching until the metal cools to maroon. Being flat, on the face of the anvil, the metal will have heat sucked out of it by the anvil, and cool quickly. Speed is essential, while taking care with accuracy. A note of warning! Do hit the punch one blow at a time; if you hit it quickly, it will bounce about, giving the surface around the hole a severe dose of square acne. The punch should be cooled every few blows, to stop it softening.

When the punch meets resistance, having gone almost through the metal, the plate should be turned over, and the punch sent through the other way. When it meets the anvil again, the plate should be put over the punch hole near the heel. The punch is then pushed through, ejecting a thin 'slug'.

Taking another heat, the punch is hit 5 times,

enlarging the hole. This will heat the punch a lot, because it is in full contact with the hot metal. It is necessary to quench the punch each time when enlarging the hole.

Withdraw the punch from the punch-hole, put the end of the punch on the surface of the anvil, and hit the hot metal, which will now be about 12 above the surface of the anvil. It will release the punch, which is immediately quenched. Turn the back plate over, and start punching from the other side. This keeps the plate flat.

Keep the hook handy, so that you can check the size of the hole for a good fit. The metal from the hole has to go somewhere. Check the sides; there is a slight swelling on each side of the plate. Inspection of the metal surrounding the hole will reveal a swelling upwards. If you get carried away and make the hole too big, you can hit this swelling, which only has one way to go – inwards – and this will reduce the size of the hole until the hook is gripped.

First curvature of ribbon scroll, showing similarity to hook snail, but this time the scroll is open.

Making the ribbon scroll

The scroll used on this hanging basket bracket is the ribbon scroll. This is the most common scroll, and the simplest. It is parallel in width, and tapered in thickness. To make the scroll, take a length of 13 × 6 × 700 long.

Heat the end, place on the anvil upright, and make a taper 40 long until the metal is a square section at the end. Take another heat, and turn the metal through a quarter turn so that it is flat on the anvil. Taper it until the end is 1.5 thick. The taper must be perfectly flat. If it has a bump, it will not bend there but at the ends of the bump. If it has a dip, it will bend at the dip. If the taper is even, it will bend evenly.

The end of the taper will have rounded slightly; make this official by rounding the end until it is a semi-circle. Next, incline the bar slightly to the side, and tap the sharp corners of the taper. These sharp corners, brought about by making the taper, are called 'arises' and should be removed. Sharp edges are undesirable, and they do not take paint very well. Each end of the bar should be tapered.

To curl the scroll, we use the small radius at the left hand end of the anvil face again. Take a heat on the taper. Place the end of the taper 6 over the radius, and very gently tap the end round, with the hammer face ending horizontal. (This is the same process as making the snail shape for the hook.) The hammer is then placed at 45 degrees, the metal is pushed forward, and made into a parabola. Another heat is taken,

Curling up the scroll enough to offer it to the scroll iron.

and the hammer placed horizontal, facing the parabola. As the left hand is raised, the hammer hits, going from horizontal to vertical, making the end of the scroll curl in – the difference between this scroll and the snail shape is that this is an open scroll.

When there is a complete curl to the scroll, it can be applied to a scroll iron to complete the amount of scroll needed. On completion, quench out the scroll, to give yourself a handle. As the scroll is an S scroll, the other end of the scroll is made in the opposite direction, and the curved length of the scroll is longer. Make the shorter scroll first, so that you have a longer handle for the second one.

End of scroll applied to the scroll iron, to roll the scroll around to the chalk mark.

The central part of the bar, which has not been curved, is straight. In traditional scroll-work, there are no straight lines. To take the straight out, we need a pair of scroll wrenches. Using a pair of flat-bit tongs, take the bar by the middle, and place in the fire, horizontally, so that the end of the curve and half of the straight are heated. You may need to juggle the bar forward and back in the fire to achieve this. Place the scroll on the face of the anvil, and, using the scroll wrenches, open up the curve

Using scroll wrenches to create curvature between scroll ends.

Scroll curved. No straight lines at all.

at the end slightly, then put a small amount of bend into the straight, getting less towards the centre of the bar, making a graceful curve. Repeat at the other end.

Now we have all of the components of the bracket.

Assembly of the bracket

To save time, the back plate can be electric-welded to the hook. There is a small space between the hook and the sides of the hole into which the weld can go and make a secure fastening. Any excess weld metal can be

ground off, making the back flat. It is important to make sure, using a set square, that the hook is perpendicular in both planes, after tacking the weld, before finishing the weld.

Check, by looking along the scroll, that the scroll is flat, not winding. If it is not flat, place the central part in the vice, tapping the scrolled part until it is flat. Offer the scroll up to the welded hook and back plate, so that it touches in three places, and mark the scroll and the bracket with chalk. Centre punch the holes, and drill the hook and back plate where the punched marks are, and drill the scroll in one place only. It is useful to have a piece of steel protruding from the drill table where the scroll can be supported for drilling. Make sure that the holes are central, as offset rivets look bad.

Scroll offered to bracket, and chalk marked where it touches.

There will be need for two different lengths of rivets, as the hook and back plate are differ-ent thicknesses. Rivet the first hole, then drill through the others, one at a time, and rivet separately, making sure that the scroll is central before drilling.

That completes the bracket, which should be painted thoroughly (better still, galvanized before painting), and should give many years' service.

Making a heel for attaching the hook

Before the advent of electric welding, many methods were used for attaching parts of iron structures. Among these was the mortise and tenon joint, as used in woodwork.

If you look at the bottom rail of an old gate, you will see a swelling near the style (upright) of the gate. This is called the heel. Part of the heel projects through the style as a mortise and tenon joint. The tenon is riveted, hot, to form the joint. The purpose of the heel is to increase the bearing area of the joint and help to prevent movement within the structure.

Heel on gate. Note swelling for heel, and riveted tenon, spread out and domed; also slight swelling where hole has been punched.

Given time and enthusiasm, the hook for the hanging basket can be attached in this way. Forming the heel necessitates upsetting the bar.

Making the tenon

Depending upon the thickness of the plate through which the tenon must go, the tenon can now be started. A cut is made with an offset chisel (or hot sett) to make a vertical face for the heel. The rest of the metal is then made into a tenon, using a sett hammer and finishing with a swage. The tenon should be in line with the hook shaft. Finally, true up the face, perpendicular to the shaft, with a monkey tool.

The mortise hole for the hook can be punched with a round punch. The tenon should protrude about its diameter through the hole.

Forging offset. Use a round-faced hammer to avoid making marks on the curve.

Cutting with butcher. This one-sided hot sett should be used with restraint; otherwise it will cut too deep, and the tenon will be cracked and break off.

UPSETTING THE HEEL

Upsetting is the last of the seven basic techniques in smithing, and probably the least used among less-experienced smiths. The smaller the section, the more likely is the material to bend; then it must be straightened before further upsetting can take place.

There are many ways to form an upset. The bar can be hit, on its end, on the anvil. With longer bars, they can be held vertically, and banged on a hard surface, such as a swage block, revolving the material with every blow.

To form the heel for a hook tenon, it is probably best to heat a short length and place horizontally in a leg vice, about 25 protruding. Make sure that the vice is very firmly closed, or the metal will be pushed along the vice, leaving ugly scars.

A large hammer – at least 1kg, preferably more – is to hand, and quick blows are rained on the end of the bar. This will almost certainly cause a bend to form, which must then be flattened on the face of the anvil. As the vice takes the heat out of the bar, it usually has to be re-heated before it can be straightened.

Three or more upsets will be needed to produce the lump to form the heel. When sufficient metal has been gathered, the swelling should be flattened on one side, until it is the same thickness as the stock size of the hook.

The resulting shape should then be forged until one side is level with the hook shaft. A round faced hammer should be used for this, to minimize marking the inside curve.

Forging upset in vice. The jaws must be fastened very tightly to stop the bar sliding along and scoring the surface.

Forging down to size with side sett.

Tenon in rough state, showing imperfections on back face, and monkey tool which is used to flatten that face.

Rivetting

To rivet together, grip the hot shaft in a vice vertically, with the face slightly above the jaws of the vice, accurately place the back pate in position, and quickly form the rivet. The thickness of the rivet head will depend upon the length of tenon protruding. If it is required to finish flush, then a countersink will be needed on the back of the plate. That concludes the making of the hanging basket bracket.

Truing up face with monkey tool, which should be revolved gently as the top is hit, ensuring right angle.

RAM'S HEAD TOASTING FORK

This job follows on from the previous ones, using many of the tools and techniques we have learned, and several extra ones. It gives the reader more variety of uses for the tools, to encourage lateral thinking.

Making the ram's head

The horns

The first part of the forging is to make the ram's horns. These are weapons in real life, and quite thick. Therefore the material we produce from our 12 square must be as thick as possible. By hammering flat on the anvil, we can reduce the thickness to 8 while widening it to 16 which gives us – when split – two sections of 8 square.

Take a piece of 12 square steel, 600 long. Heat the end, and place 80 over the face of the anvil. Hit vigorously to make it flat, checking that it does not reduce below 8 thick. Do not hit the sides of the metal at all. It should make 16 wide.

Now place half of the flattened metal over the beak, and taper the end down to 10×3. By tapering at this stage, it reduces the amount of work needed to taper the horns after splitting. Make sure that the taper is offset, so that one

OPPOSITE: **Ram's head: bar tapered and offset before splitting the horns.**

face is flat. The flattened part is now split, using a hot sett. If necessary, cool the flat, and mark carefully with a cold chisel, to ensure that the split is central. (Remember the cutting of the back plate in Chapter 7.)

Start the split at the widest part of the flat. Again, remember the heavier hammer, and the carefully placed sett with single blows. Extra marks alongside the main cut are not wanted. Remember, too, the thin plate under the metal when the sett is going through. The sett should go through right to the end of the split.

When the split is completed, place the hot bar in the vice with the split protruding. Take the hot sett, and lever the two parts apart. The edges where the sett went through will be raggy. Turn the bar over, and file off the rags. They could be forged into the surface, but these horns are going to be twisted, and the rags would emerge, like little razor blades, and that

Prising horns apart after splitting.

Filing away the rough ragged parts left after splitting.

part is going to be the handle. So early removal saves work – and hands – later on.

The two parts of the horns are now in trapezoid section. We need to square them up. Heat the horns, and place at the edge of the anvil. Hit the other end of the bar, to widen the horns apart. The longest side of the trapezoid section needs compressing. Place the horn over the anvil edge, and lean the bar into the longest side. Hit the bar at the longest side, and it will compress,

making the bar square. If it twists, straighten up by hitting flat on the anvil, and lean it more into the longest side. Hammer the horn square. Try not to hammer too much, as this will thin out the horn and make the result effeminate. After squaring up, taper the very end down to 1.5 square. Always make the end of a scroll really fine; otherwise it will not curl up completely at the end. Lumpy scroll ends are ugly.

Next bring the two horns together. They should be the same length to within 12 of each other. If they are not, cut some off the longer, and draw the end out again to the fine point. Once together, a cut should be made halfway through the bar, 30 behind the cut made by the hot sett, on the same side as the original direction of that division. The fact that the cut is there determines that the bar will bend at that point. If you try to bend the bar without the cut, it might bend where you want it to, but sometimes the steel appears to have a mind of its own, and bends 'somewhere near' your desired location. The end with the horns is then bent back on itself.

Welding the head

The next part of the making of the ram's head is to weld the two parts of the head into one.

Leaning the split horn into the longer side, to avoid twisting out of shape when hit.

The tapered bars brought together, and cut half way through to make the bar bend where you want it. It's important to make this cut from the same side as the split.

FIRE WELDING PRACTICE

Practice the technique of welding before trying it out on the finished item. There is no mystique to it, and if the instructions are followed, to the letter, the weld will take – it will be successful.

Remove clinker

First, clean any clinker out of the fire. Welding needs to be done in a clean fire. Any traces of clinker, however small, will impair the welding ability of the steel. It is best to let the fire cool for five minutes before removing clinker. This is because, when hot, it is slightly liquid, and cooling it consolidates the clinker into a single piece. There is less chance of particles distributing themselves throughout the fire if it is in one piece. After cooling the fire, gently scrape the hot coke off the top to the side, and lever up the clinker with the poker. Slide the shovel under the clinker, and put it to the side of the fire to cool, before putting it in the bin. Recompose the fire, and raise the blast.

Divide the bar

Take a piece of scrap bar, the same section as the ram's head bar, and heat the end. Mark across the metal at 30 from the end (the same length as the proposed face on the ram). Cut it halfway through at this point, and bend it back on itself, checking that the meeting surfaces are clean.

Bring up to heat

Check where the diagonals cross on the fire. This will be the hottest part of the fire. Make sure that the fire is a shallow conical shape, and put the end into the fire, short part uppermost, about 50 above the tue. After a minute, make a little hole in the top of the fire, so that you can see the metal within. It should be orange by now. Watch out for little white bursting sparks coming out of the fire. That is the first indication that it is getting up to heat. Look at the upper surface of the metal; it should have small dark areas, which are oxide. When the metal is up to heat, these dark areas will turn liquid, and the surface will look wet. It is ready.

Draw it out of the fire quickly, place upon the anvil, and hit sharply. Lots of sparks will fly off the metal. Hit it a few times, not too hard, turn and hit the sides, and stop. Turn the fire down.

Testing

To test the weld, place the short end in the vice, with the main stem out of the vice, and pull gently towards you. If the metal bends after the weld, it has taken. If it bends at the end of the metal, it has not. It is best to try this a few times before taking on the real thing.

Prepared practice piece, and welded practice head, before features are added.

The face

After welding together successfully, you need to practise making the face. A ram's face is quite long, and not very tapered, unlike a deer's. The weld needs, therefore, to be tapered from two thicknesses of the bar, to one.

Take another heat, and place the tapered face on the anvil, with the diagonal upward. Hit this to make a facet on the side of the face. When this is done on both sides, it creates a ridge down the nose. The next phase is to round off the nose into a hemisphere, so place the nose next to the far edge of the anvil, and tap gently around the nose, while revolving the bar.

The face is now ready for its features. Take an eye punch, or a centre punch, and position it on the facet, about 20 from the nose, at 45 degrees. Drive the punch into the metal, in the case of the eye punch gathering up some metal to make the eyeball. Then raise the punch while hitting it, and revolving to create the eyeball. Repeat at the other side. Next take the centre punch, and make a small impression in each eyeball for the pupils.

Take another heat, and make some larger holes in the end of the nose, for nostrils. The hot sett is used then for making the mouth beneath the nostrils. Make the cut go around the side of the face, to create the impression of grinning. Practise this a few times before attempting the real thing.

When you are ready to do the head, clean the fire again, and follow the instructions as before. When it is welded, it is time to make the neck.

Eye punch, showing hollow hemisphere.

Eye punch in position, 20 from end of nose.

The neck

Take the anvil fork, and place in the hardie hole. Heat the metal, and when it is orange, put the face into the fork, with the eye just next to the upright of the fork; draw the stem back, around the fork, until it almost touches the chin. Take the metal off the fork, replace it the other way round and pull back to make the second bend.

Head in position, eyeball just to the side of the fork.

Head removed from fork and reversed, to make neck.

Twisting the horns

Heat the horns gently. Remember that they are thin, and therefore vulnerable. The horns will also cool quickly, because the ratio of surface area to volume is higher. In order to minimize the cooling effect of contact with the tongs, give the tongs a preheat in the fire for about ten seconds, to take the chill off.

After heating, place the neck in the vice with the horns horizontal. Take the flat bit tongs and twist each side outwards, about three quarter turns. Remember they twist in opposite directions.

Quenching the beginning of the horn and the head. This stops the head conducting any heat to the horn, and prevents the overheated part of the horn from twisting off.

At this point, quench the head completely. As the head has a smaller ratio of surface area to

Head clamped in the vice, with horns pointing to right. Heated flat bit tongs are used to make twist.

Scroll tongs, used to roll up the horns into a flat scroll.

volume, and will cool more slowly, conducting heat into the horn, which will twist more where it is hottest. If you do not quench, the horn can twist off irreparably. It is almost impossible to weld a horn back at that point, because you cannot get the weld inside.

Having cooled the head, the part of the horn which is to be twisted is then heated as necessary, and twisting continues right up to the end. Do them separately.

Rolling up the horns

This part of the operation is achieved with another set of tongs, which are called scroll tongs or round pliers (mentioned in Chapter 5). Remember that the end of the horn is very fine,

Using bow pliers to regularize the scroll of the horns.

so turn down the fire. Heat the end, and take the very end of the horn and turn it, so that there is no straight line at the end. Move the tongs along, and turn some more. After a turn or two, the metal has become thicker, so it will be necessary to take a different grip to use the leverage of the reins (handles). Continue until the whole of the horn is curled up. Repeat on the other horn.

Regularizing the horn

Yet another pair of tongs is now needed: the bow pliers. These are used with both hands, and they bring the scroll of the horns into a

Using bolt tongs to hold the shaft for tapering.

regular form, with even gaps all along the length. A shallow cone should be formed when the horn is finished.

That completes the ram's head. We next make the rest of the toasting fork.

Forging the fork

Tapering the shaft

Below the head and neck, there will be a twist, of which later. Below the twist, the shaft tapers a long way, until it spreads out and becomes the fork. The twist is left until later because that part of the shaft has to be gripped by yet another set of tongs – the bolt tongs. These go over the head and grip the shaft below the neck. If the metal were twisted, the bolt tongs could make marks on the edges of the twist. As it is, they grip the flats of the bar.

Triangular joint formed between shaft and fork, before splitting.

Before commencing the taper, make centre punch marks on all four sides where the twist will ultimately be. The tapering is started just below the lower marks. Heat the bar and place upon the beak to draw the taper down. It will take several heats, though the amount of drawing down is considerably less than the former exercises. You should leave about 75 untouched at the lower end of the bar. This will be used to make the fork later. The section at the lower end of the taper should be about 8 square, and the join should be curved.

From the work on the beak, the surface will be uneven. Now heat the bar, and smooth the faces of the bar with a flat hammer. This will create arises, which need to be removed gently.

The fork tines

The square on the end of the shaft is now flattened on the face of the anvil. It should, as with the horns, become 16 × 8. Again, half of its length should be tapered to 10 × 3, and it should be split. It is very important that the split is central, for the appearance of the finished fork. The triangular join from the shaft should also be untouched as it adds considerably to the appearance of the fork. The end of the split should be carefully marked, to miss cutting into the triangle.

On completing the split, take a pair of vice 'cheeks' and support the triangle in them. The tines (prongs) of the fork can then be hammered down flat, while the cheeks prevent the vice from 'galling' the right angle. Take from the vice, lay flat on the anvil, flatten any twists and file off any rags. The tines should now be squared off, as the horns were, leaning into the longest edge before hammering. The ends should be quite fine. It is very important that the tines are exactly the same length, which should be about 110 long. If one is longer, slightly more than the difference should be cut off with the hardie, and the fine taper restored. Remove the arises along the tines.

Vice cheeks supporting triangle, preventing galling of metal. These pieces of angle steel have a radius ground on the edge, and a longer radius on the inside surface to accommodate the triangle.

Place the tines across the beak, at about 50 diameter and tap one of them gently over the beak, slightly past a right angle. Turn the whole shaft round, so that the straight tine is over the same part of the beak, and curve this one. The ends of the tines should now be tapped over the top of the beak outwards, creating a double curve.

Twisting

Cool out the fork, to use it as a handle. Heat the top of the bar, beneath the neck, where the

punch marks are. Join the punch marks with a line, cut by the hot sett. It needs to be about 1.5 deep.

When all four faces are grooved, heat the bar evenly – all the same colour – over the length of the grooves, and grip above the lower end of the groove in the vice. Take a pair of tongs – preferably open jawed – and grip above the twist. Turn the bar through one and a half turns. Check for alignment.

Remove from the vice, and check for straightness. It will usually be bent. If the twist is bent,

Twisting with wrench. To ensure an even twist metal must be all the same colour.

Straightening with scroll wrench.

place the untwisted part in the vice, and take a scroll wrench to the other end, and gently bend it straight. If this means that the straight part above the twist is now at an angle, place the twist very gently in the vice (carefully avoiding marking the edges of the twist with the jaws), and straighten with the scroll wrench. Repeat for the other plane.

Setting the curves in the other plane with a round-faced hammer.

Setting the fork

The last job is to set the curvature of the fork as seen from the side. For this job, we use a round-faced hammer.

Take a gentle heat on the tines and the adjacent 75 of the shaft. Juggle the fork through the fire if necessary to get an even heat. It only needs to be red. Place the tines of the fork at an angle on the face of the anvil, and tap the end at each side with the round-faced hammer. Tap further up, each side, until a gentle curve is formed. Turn the fork over, place the triangular part at the edge of the anvil, and tap a curve into the end of the shaft. Check the tines for alignment.

That concludes the forging of the fork.

Finished curvature of toasting fork.

Finishing

To finish, wire brush vigorously, preferably while it is still hot. If there are blemishes caused by adhering scale or clinker, they might have to be removed by heating to yellow hot, when they can be brushed off easily. (For some reason, the scale stays on at red and orange heats.) After brushing, the surface should be covered with some protection.

Wax

For indoors, at domestic humidity, a wax finish is adequate but must be renewed at intervals, depending upon the ambient humidity. There are many types of wax suitable for finishing ironwork. However, it should be borne in mind that all organic waxes do, ultimately, oxidize. This means that they turn brown. On 'antique' iron, this is an advantage, but it can spoil the effect if a metallic look is required.

Waxes can, after application, be heated to blacken them. Bees wax goes really black, but the slightest over-application can cause the wax to go crusty and lumpy. Linseed oil goes black, but gives off a dreadful smell during heating, and finishes dark brown. Mansion polish – a furniture polish for wood or floors – goes on well, and gives an even black finish if heated to the correct temperature (experiment to find it), and the finish is durable. It contains carnauba wax.

Renaissance wax is recommended for a finish that does not go brown and does not need heating. It was first developed by the museum industry some years ago. It is used for metal, wood, leather and other substances. Crystal-line, non-organic, it spreads sparingly, and gives a pleasant feel when polished. Like many waxes, it builds up with a few applications. It is not impervious to damp conditions, and rust can form on the surface. If caught quickly, the rust can be wiped off, before another coat is applied.

Galvanizing

For outdoor protection, galvanizing is one of the best treatments. The process involves pick-ling the metal in dilute sulphuric acid, which dissolves any scale and rust, and gets the metal completely clean. It is then washed in clean water, to remove the acid, and dipped in a flux to assist adhesion of the zinc. The last stage is to dip it into molten zinc for a few minutes. There is a surface transfer of molecules between the steel and the zinc, and a deposit of zinc about 60 microns thick on the surface of the steel.

Apart from the physical protection of the zinc, in case of surface damage there is further protection by 'galvanic action', where the zinc acts as a 'sacrifice' and oxidizes itself rather than the steel. Even without a paint finish, the galvanizing should protect the steel for 25 years.

If there are any hollow sections, they must be drilled in order for air to be released. The temperature of the galvanizing bath is 460° and any air trapped inside can cause an explosion. The zinc therefore goes inside the job, and adds to the protection. A drawback to this method is that acid can be trapped in between sections and not washed away before dipping. This can result in rusty stains around the trapped acid.

Fresh zinc will not hold ordinary paint, as it is quite greasy, but there are various ways of applying paint after galvanizing. A mordant solution will etch the surface, and enable red oxide primer to be applied, and after drying, the undercoat and top coat. Recent develop-ments in paint technology have produced coat-ings which can be applied direct to fresh galva-nizing, but they must be sprayed.

Shot blasting

Another method is to have the whole job shot blasted, and sprayed with molten zinc. This gives the metal a slightly rough surface, an excellent key for paint finishes, which are usually sprayed on and give a smooth surface.

Primer and undercoat

If none of the above technology is available, the surface to be protected must be vigorously wire brushed, and a good metal primer brushed on.

Primer is usually red, but might be grey. It is better to start with red, because ironwork is very hard to completely cover. Using rubber gloves to protect hands, turn the ironwork through 90 degrees and look for the missed parts. With red paint, these will be immediately visible. Turn 90 degrees again, and you will see some more, and again. Then turn the job vertically and do the same at the other side. That is eight times!

This process should be repeated with grey undercoat, and black (or any other finishing colour) top coat. It is a long job. For this reason, if you are giving a quote for a job, ensure you ask lots for painting jobs. I was toldmany years ago that clerks of work inspecting finishes always carried a stick with a mirror attached, with which to view the underside of gate rails, as most painters paint what they can see.

Bitumen

If setting galvanized posts into concrete, give the part to be submerged two coats of bitumen-based paint before setting. Concrete has a corrosive effect on steel, even if galvanized.

T-wash

Another, quite attractive durable finish is galvanizing which has been treated with a mordant solution (often referred to as T-wash). This gives the surface a grey, uneven texture, which gradually darkens with age.

Bead blasting

For indoor use only, the surface of the iron/ steel can be bead blasted to remove all oxide, and then allowed to rust all over. If this is then rubbed down and waxed, that gives it a pleasant finish.

ACKNOWLEDGEMENTS

My first thanks go to my friend, David Tucker, who was originally to have written this book, with minor contributions from me, but whose other commitments precluded his spending the necessary time on it.

My second thanks go to the late J.K. Powell, who was my tutor in 'Craft' at the College of the Venerable Bede, Durham, in the 1960s. He had only one standard – excellence – which I have always attempted to achieve. It was the pursuit of this which led me to travel far and wide to see, first hand, examples of craftsmanship in various media, and to appreciate the accumulated skills that created it.

Thirdly, I thank Jack Summers, who worked 'next door' for twenty-plus years. Jack served his time as a blacksmith during the war in his uncle's shop at Hayden Bridge, Northumberland, acquiring generations' worth of knowledge, dating back to time immemorial. On completing his apprenticeship, Jack went to work in Seaton Delaval Colliery. This entailed shoeing ponies underground, and working in the 'top shop' doing the engineering blacksmiths' work. There, again, he had the benefit of five generations of experience, from men who all vied to be the best in the shop. The last thirty years of his industrial work were spent in the steel industry – where he originally felt like a fish out of water – and he ended up working a two-ton hammer. Tales of these times were recalled each lunch time as we sat next to the anvil and the fire every day. He showed me many of the techniques that I'm passing on in this book.

Thanks also go to the various curators of Preston Hall Museum, part of Stockton-on-Tees Borough Council, who have permitted me over the last thirty-five years, or so, to metamorphose from teacher to blacksmith in the blacksmiths shop in their Victorian Street. There too, I have been enabled to teach smithing to curious beginners, some of whom have gone on to take up the craft, both as a hobby and full-time.

Lastly, I thank my wife, Janice, who bravely encouraged me in my transition from a regular income to almost permanent 'doing without' – especially in the early days – as I'm no businessman. To my family, too, who had to exist without my presence, as I was always working at weekends, I apologize. And without my son, Chris, this book could not have happened, as my ability to use modern technology is very limited. So grateful thanks to him.

INDEX